David Cooper

Table of Contents

INTRODUCTION

Social anxiety and shyness are common signs of a struggle with self-esteem and confidence. Social anxiety occurs when any form of social interaction causes severe nervousness, anxiety, and fear. This can happen when we anticipate meeting a new acquaintance or co-worker, or it can be experienced prior to family gatherings or seeing someone we know. Attending a conference, party or event can cause signs of anxiety. Situations that require social interaction can bring about a sense of dread, and as a result, many people who experience social anxiety have avoided social situations completely. It is estimated that around 8-10 percent of the population is affected by chronic social anxiety, whereas up to more than half of people will experience aspects of social anxiety in their lifetime at least on occasion, and usually during childhood. The fear of meeting a new schoolteacher or avoiding conflict with other kids at school may be examples of what may ignite fear or cause stress or uncertainty. For most people, social anxiety is often associated with extreme circumstances that are likely to cause fear, such as attending a court hearing or having to face someone who is abusive. For nearly ten percent of the population, social anxiety and shyness is a constant that can hinder development in friendships, work and how we interact with people in general.

Other struggles or challenges faces with social anxiety include low self- esteem and a lack of confidence. Self-esteem is defined as self-respect and confidence in one's abilities and having a sense of worth or value, also known as self-confidence. When we lack this sense of value in ourselves, it impacts every part of our life. For some people, they may be keenly aware of their feelings of inadequacy, while others may not recognize them immediately. may feel inadequate around other people, as if they do not measure up to …

The Symptoms and Characteristics of Social Anxiety

What are the symptoms or characteristics of social anxiety? When we feel anxious in a social situation, clammy or sweaty hands, an increased heart rate and shallow breathing are some of the signs we experience. It can happen hours or even days before an interaction or meeting with people. The anticipation can be a major reason for these symptoms, as our mind, when stressed, tends to exaggerate or magnify the situation as more of an obstacle than it is. Even when we are aware of our exaggerated response or reaction, it can still be difficult to adjust our thinking and reduce stress.

When these characteristics are frequent, the toll on our nervous system and mental health can be exhausting. As a result, we might avoid social contact whenever these symptoms begin. Just the thought of a social gathering or party can trigger sweaty palms, for example, and make us feel nervous immediately. When avoiding contact with people, it's to alleviate or stop the symptoms of our anxiety as well. As both the symptoms and the fear of socializing become more frequent, we withdraw further and do as much as possible to limit the triggering effect. In the long-term, this can become severe in limiting our progress in and enjoyment of life.

The Social Anxiety and Self-Esteem Connection

Shyness and fear of social interaction are intricately linked to how we view and value ourselves. We may often chastise our actions or performance or become critical for our physical appearance.; our inner voice is the product of others' comments and feedback: if we were bullied or criticized as children, we internalize those messages and replay them as our "inner voice". When an employer or parent always tells us that we're not doing enough, we hear that on repeat in our mind. The impact of how other people and society sees us or perceived as seeing us is monumental to how we view ourselves. When we feel negative about our self-image, we automatically expect that other people will do the same, hence the avoidance of social interaction.

How can self-esteem or confidence be improved? There are practical exercises that can help us recognize how we view ourselves and overcome excessive negative and critical thoughts. This begins with our way of thinking. Taking action to address sources of negative or destructive thinking is an important step to making progress. The following exercises can prove very helpful in making us aware of our own thinking:

1.   Make a list of positive traits. Write at least ten positive things you can think of. When we look in the mirror, we immediately criticize certain details: we may be unhappy with our complexion or hair or wish to lose weight. When we make a habit of doing this, it defeats any intention of becoming more positive. Keep in mind personality traits, abilities and other attributes in addition to your appearance. Think of the pleasant things people

have mentioned to you. For example, you may struggle with body image, but receive compliments on your sense of style. You may not be good at solving complex math equations, though you can be creative, and good at finding solutions.

2.   Think about the traits or characteristics you like about yourself. Think exclusively about what you like, not what others say. This is a good exercise in switching the negative voice in our mind to a more positive one. Some people are fixated on their errors and forget to take time to appreciate their accomplishments.

3.   Skills and achievements. Thinks of any accomplishments you have achieved and write them down. Choose at least five. Consider your achievements at work, school or within your family. Finishing a project, learning a new skill or sport are examples of skills. It doesn't have to be a large-scale project or goal; it can be something as simple as trying a new recipe or renovating

a room in your house. Educational and career milestones are important, though don't overlook smaller, significant achievements, such as learning a new gardening technique or reading a book. We often get caught up in everyday life to the point where the smaller things get ignored, and yet they can bring us joy and give us a sense of satisfaction.

4.   Overcoming difficult situations. Everyone is faced with a challenging situation where they have no choice but to act to resolve or mitigate a solution. This can be anything from a tight deadline at work to coping with an unpleasant person or stressful event where we find ourselves in a "fight or flight" response mode. Think of at least three situations where you were confronted with such a situation and how you were able to successfully navigate through it. Getting through such an occurrence doesn't have to be heroic, such as saving someone from a car accident or verbally confronting a bully. It can be as simple as facing fear and using techniques, such as deep breathing, to remain calm until you find inner calm.

5.   When we experience social anxiety, we often feel alone and this can be unbearable for many people, who crave human contact. Even when we are surrounded by family, friends, and people who seem genuine, we may feel alone. We may focus only on the critical things people say to us. Try to focus and think of at least four or five people who have helped you. This may be easier than you realize, as even people we see as unfriendly, may be experiencing challenges of their own, and yet they can surprise us with a kind gesture or comment. An act of kindness, however big or small, makes the most impact on a person who really needs a sense of hope. When you consider the people you help you think less of what they actually did and more about their intentions behind it.

In creating these lists, take your time and reflect on your decisions. What about each of these items makes them significant enough that they are chosen? The purpose of the exercise is not just finding positive things to list, but also to reflect on each of them carefully, and enjoy the positivity for each experience. Building self-esteem is a long process, especially if we have always had difficulty with confidence. Results will not appear overnight, though keeping our minds on as many positive characteristics and attributes about ourselves is a much healthier approach.

CHAPTER 1

MANAGE SOCIAL ANXIETY

Techniques to Reduce Stress and Anxiety Before a Job Interview, Meeting, and Everyday Situations

When considering the types of scenarios that cause us to experience social anxiety, we may think of specific events or situations such as public speaking, meeting a new person or people or going to a job interview. For some people, only certain experiences cause panic, while others feel natural and routine. For some people, anxiety may occur before more everyday experiences, such as approaching a salesclerk in a store or asking for directions. There are steps that can help you overcome everyday scenarios:

1.   Consider the average, everyday situation that requires social interaction. This could be a simple task of asking a random bystander for directions to a restaurant

or when a train will arrive. Other scenarios that are simple though may cause nervousness may be greeting co-workers at a company gathering or approaching your employer to ask a question about your job. Thinking about these and similar scenarios, keep the following in mind:

a.   All interactions are simple and brief. Take a deep breath and think of what to say before you proceed. This can be as simple as "Hello, how are you?" or "Good morning, do you happen to know when the next train is due?" Even a light smile and nod is a great way to acknowledge someone in a friendly way, without making them feel uncomfortable.

b.   All these brief conversations are positive or neutral in nature. They should not cause an argument, nor should they evoke an unreasonable response. If, or some reason, a people reacts or responds in a disrespectful manner, or ignores you, simply find someone else who may be able to help. If a co-worker or acquaintance displays a negative attitude, take it in stride, and move on.

c.   Realistically, most people will respond in a reasonable manner. If you are polite and kind, expect the same in response. More often, people are either neutral or will speak like us when they answer a question or provide information.

2.   If the thought of approaching a stranger in an unfamiliar place causes you to feel nervousness or anxiety, consider speaking with someone who is in a position to help. For example, an "Information" booth in a tourist area of a new city or town is a great place to start. Visiting a gas station, general store or approaching a security guard in a shopping center are good candidates to ask for directions, ideas on where places are best to shop or eat and other typical, easy information. Most people in these situations are knowledgeable, or they can point you in the right direction to find what you are

looking for.

3.   If speaking to someone face-to-face is too much to handle in a specific situation, make a phone call instead. Sending an instant message or email can also work, though responses are not always immediate. Speaking over the phone is a way to get in contact with someone fast and communicate effectively. If you are prone to stumbling over what to say at the moment, prepare what you plan to say or ask first, which may include writing it down so that the words flow easier. Calling or emailing someone before you meet them is another way to make the transition easier to "in person". Chances are even greater that the interaction will be pleasant and go smoothly. For example, if you plan to visit a new store, call ahead to speak with a salesclerk and inquire about a few products and/or service. Let them know when you plan to arrive if ask if they are willing to help. This will go a long way to putting you at ease and bridge the gap between familiar and unknown.

Preparing for a Meeting or Job Interview

One of the most stressful events that most people dread is the job interview. The first time you meet a prospective employer, it's all about first impressions: your resume, cover letter, skill set, and your appearance. The very thought of making a good first impression can be stressful, especially when we are hard on ourselves and often find fault with our performance.

When you prepare for an interview or any important meeting with a person or group of people, it's a time to "shine" and promote your strengths and sell your abilities. In other meetings, such as community groups for a volunteer project or similar events, many of these tips and ideas applied to preparing for a job interview may apply:

1.   Review the expectations of the job. Read, and become familiar with the qualifications and duties are for the position. There may be a list of attributes or specific

skills needed, or a more open- ended variety of characteristics for a job. Knowing what the expectations and if they match your experience and skills is important, even before you apply to the job.

2.   Research the company or organization. Knowing about a company's history, products and/or services is vital. During an interview, you may be asked why you want to work for a company or join an organization. It's important to know the "why" and explain it in simple, but effective terms, for example:

a.   "I would like to work for this company/volunteer for this organization because I respect the values of the organization and am a goal-oriented person."
b.   "I feel that my skill-set and experience can contribute positively to the goals of the company/organization." When you are able to express, in one or two sentences, why you would make a good fit for a company and indicate that you have done the research, not only will you

feel more confident in yourself, you will also instill a level of confidence in you with the prospective employer or team members about your abilities.

3.   Create a portfolio of your achievements, experience, and education. A current, relevant resume is important, as well as a brief, and direct cover letter. To build confidence in yourself, take an inventory of your achievements: certificates, courses, volunteer positions and other goals that can be compiled and filed into a binder or book for easy reference. This is a good reference and reminder of what you are capable of and can accomplish. Depending on the type of interview or meeting you prepare for, you may or may not bring this along, though it is a good way to keep your spirits up and maintain a positive outlook on your value and self-worth.

4.   Dress well and professionally. Most places of employment or organizations that require volunteers have a relaxed, semi-casual dress policy. Even where an

environment is very open to most forms of attire, dress professionally. Aim high for a good first impression. If you are not comfortable in very formal attire, a plain, well-fitted pair of pants and crisp blouse or shirt can do the trick, along with a comfortable pair of dress shoes. Professional doesn't have to be expensive, elaborate or to impress, as your abilities and achievements will do the work.

Preparing ahead will naturally reduce anxiety and pressure associated with impending social or professional meetings and situations. Keep in mind that the people you meet with may be nervous as well; often we forget that other people may experience the same or similar feelings of anxiousness or uncertainty. Knowing as much as possible beforehand will make a big difference in how you confident you feel. The more we know about a specific topic, the more likely we are to feel comfortable to talk about it openly and without hesitation.

When a meeting or interview is completed, you may feel

a sense of relief. A social interaction, for people with chronic anxiety, can be very exhausting. The amount of courage and preparation can be daunting and not knowing the outcome of the event, or what may follow, can make us feel uneasy. Take time to relax and give yourself credit. Getting through an interview, meeting or social event is not an easy task for everyone, and if you find yourself feeling drained emotional afterward, take time for you and focus on your needs. Enjoy a delicious meal, watch a movie or visit a nearby park to enjoy the scenery, and most of all, reward yourself with a job well done.

Suggestions and Practical Exercises for Starting Good Conversations

When we prepare ahead for the interview, the party or the dinner with a few co-workers, we're setting up a positive stage for a successful social interaction. Once we get to the event, however, there can be challenges beyond the initial greetings and small talk. If we are in a social setting where the other people are new to us, starting a conversation can be a challenge. A group of co-workers or friends may already share a lot in common and jump into a discussion about a television show, food trends, current news or other topics that they have talked about before and share common interests.

Starting a new conversation can seem impossible when everyone else already knows what to talk about, and sometimes the topics they enjoy may not align with ours. It's important to keep in mind that social interaction always changes. One topic will change to another, and not everybody will share the same point of view. When you are new to a group, making a friendly connection is a goal we work towards, and this will indicate which individual(s) are easy to communicate and share ideas with. Some conversations can be very lively, humorous and exciting, while others may seem boring, uneventful or uninteresting. Starting a good conversation is important, especially when meeting people for the first time, as it gives them a first impression of how we communicate and the types of interests we have. Not every conversation will be continuous, and after a few exchanges, it may end quickly, and we can simply move on to other people and begin again. Taking the initiative to begin a conversation can be a big step for people who are usually shy or experience social anxiety. The key is to keep the introduction simple and light-hearted:

- Talk about the weather. Everybody does it and is aware of the forecast. It's one of the easiest topics to talk about and a great conversation starter. If you know about a possible storm warning or downpour, even better. Take note that after a few comments about whether it's going to rain or snow, most people will stop at that point, and decide to change to another topic. As an opener, though, it's a neutral and common topic that anyone can relate to. Introduce yourself. If you are at a friend's party or meeting new people at work or local community function, make a point to simply walk up to someone and say "Hi, my name is_____".

Offer to shake hands or simply nod when making the exchange. Not everyone will shake hands, and some people will graciously accept a handshake. Following the introduction, ask the person how they are and/or if they are having a good time. This is a positive way to engage and make both them and you feel comfortable with the interaction. This also gives you a chance to learn about people, their names and maybe something about them after the initial greeting.

-Use a person's name in the conversation, even if only once after the introduction. This can apply to a simple greeting that lasts less than a minute, or a longer conversation of five minutes or more.

When a person tells you their name, respond with "It's a pleasure to meet you,_____". Not only does the response indicate that you are paying attention to them, but it also makes them feel special and recognized, if only by name. It is an excellent way to network for business connections and building relationships in a certain field of work.

Be witty or funny. This may not be the best option for everyone. If the idea of taking a chance on being funny doesn't seem like a good fit for you, them avoid it altogether. If you are familiar with widely accepted styles of humor and feel comfortable sharing a quick joke or pun, go for it. It's a bit riskier than a formal introduction, but it is ideal in a casual or semi-formal setting where people tend to be more relaxed and personable, and less about business. A witty joke, pun or riddle that is light and jovial is the best option for opening a fun conversation.

Talk about music or sports. These are easy topics that most people are interested in. If a person is not keen on following sports teams or who is winning a particular game, simply switch to music. The same can be done in the reverse. With either music, sports or both, you're likely to get some feedback on different kinds of sports, teams, musicians, and concerts. Sports and arts, in general, evoke a lot of passion from some people, and this can be a positive step in having a rewarding conversation and future discussions, especially where you find common interests. You may discover that both of you attended the same concert or enjoy the same types of music. If there is a sports game playing at an event or music, these topics become even easier to engage in.

Be genuine. Sometimes when we are nervous, we overdo it. We might take that deep breath and over-exert our efforts to engage with the conversation. It might interest some people if they see us as enthusiastic and positive, or it may scare them away if we come across as too bold. The best way to avoid this occurrence is to keep it real and genuine. Just be yourself and don't sound too rehearsed. If you become so nervous that you get tongue-tied, just say "hi" or "hello". That's as easy as it gets, and it's not going to be awkward. It also opens the opportunity to more conversation and friendly interaction in general.

A lot of people we encounter in social situations may come across as confident, well-poised and smooth in conversation. We may not realize that some of these people work hard to master these skills and could also experience social anxiety. In other words, not everyone with social anxiety will approach communication in the same manner. Some people will go "all or nothing", where they either remain withdrawn and quiet, then suddenly spark a conversation with someone. They may have been mentally preparing for a while, waiting for the right moment, when they feel most at ease. For others, it's a slow, but steady process of making small talk in brief conversations. It varies for everyone, and the most important goal is to take the plunge and make that initial contact.

Dealing with Rejection in an Initial Conversation

It's not easy to accept rejection, and in fact, most people will avoid meeting new people and social engagements altogether for the sole purpose of avoiding the possibility of being rejected. Starting a new conversation, when you have social anxiety, is a big step that takes a lot of courage and sometimes, a lot of mental and emotional preparation. If someone simply "waves" us away or ignores us, it cuts deep. It hurts and makes us feel inadequate and unworthy to talk to. It's important to realize that when this happens, there are many reasons why people do this. When rejection occurs in the initial stage of the conversation, right at the beginning, it's not something to take personally. Sometimes people are experiencing an emotion or feeling related to another incident or situation that we are not aware of. If this happens to you, simply smile, nod and move on. You did your best by making an effort, and that is all you need to do. Even the most social conversationalists will be rejected if someone simply isn't in the mood to talk.

During a conversation, we may begin to feel relaxed and comfortable with someone, and then rejection happens. It can be a simple reason, such as a distraction, or another person may join in the conversation and "take over". Some people can be easily put off by certain topics, even non-controversial ones, simply because they lack interest. Realistically, there are people who simply do not practice kindness and can behave impolitely. In order to know what to expect in any social situation, always expect that at least one person will behave this way simply because that's who they are. It usually has no bearing on who you are or the conversation itself, and the rejection-like behavior may stem from something completely unrelated. Every now and then, people will simply pass judgment at first glance and not want to speak at all. If they become rude and offensive, simply leave the conversation and do not engage any further. This happens to everyone. We all have to deal with difficult, challenging people, regardless of how friendly we are or how much we want to get along. Some people are just not willing to be kind or fair. Take the high road and avoid them, without any further discussion. If possible, take yourself away from the social event, and take a walk outside.

When (and if) you return, and feel comfortable in doing so, try having a conversation with someone who you have conversed with before and have already established a good rapport. Rejection is not an easy experience to deal with, but it can help us learn to cope with difficult people and situations. As much as socializing is important, recognizing when to leave a situation and take time or self-care is equally, if not more important. Self-confidence is a delicate matter for many people, especially for those of us who experience social anxiety. For this reason, never hesitate or feel guilty for leaving a conversation or social group if you feel uncomfortable in any way or form.

Pitfalls to Avoid in Conversations

Knowing how to start a conversation and engage with others is important and vital to establishing good communication skills. It's just as vital to avoid certain behaviors and tactics that can cause arguments and grief, especially if you don't really know the person and would like to get to know them more.

Some topics, for example, should be avoided altogether, until you know whether or not they are appropriate. The typical avoidance of "religion and politics" is a good rule of thumb, as well as certain current news items that may also shift easily towards religion and/or politics. There are exceptions: if you attend an event specific to a topic that may normally be contentious, but it involves a shared point of view because of a specific occasion or event, then it may actually be a good topic of discussion. For example, if you attend a political event or volunteer for a specific organization that promotes equality and/or specific values that align with your views, it can be reasonably expected that other people who participate in the same event would share those same beliefs and/or values. In these instances, a politically charged conversation may be a worthwhile experience!

Don't get too personal. Some people are comfortable sharing their past, previous relationships and many other topics that are very personal and sometimes embarrassing. If you don't know someone well, avoid topics of conversation that are too personal. This includes romantic relationships, past relationships, family struggles, and health conditions. Even if you stick with regular, non-personal conversations, you may still find that some items

should not be included. If you notice someone's facial expression changing, and they move away at the mere mention of a certain item, change the topic right away. For example, some people are comfortable talking about sexuality in general (not personal), while others avoid it completely. As a general rule, don't discuss anything personal unless you know the person well, and are familiar with their level of comfort when it comes to different topics of conversation.

Being confident and improving your self-esteem is one of the primary goals to overcoming social anxiety, though once we become more confident, we may want to talk more about ourselves and our achievements. This is a great way to find things in common with other people, however, dominating a conversation and making it all about you can drive the other person or people away. People will be genuinely interested in you, and may even ask questions about your job, family, vacations and other topics. When you talk about yourself, make sure to reciprocate and ask the other for something that concerns them to maintain their interest. Some people are good listeners, but they also want to converse and keep the conversation going both ways.

Listen to what other people have to say. You will learn a lot about a person by how they talk, not only in their verbal expression but non-verbal cues as well. When you take the time to listen to someone else, you will also get a sense of who they are and what interests them, which in turn, helps you engage with them even more. If we spend more time talking than listening, it only takes longer to get to know someone else. Listening helps build a bridge of understanding and people tend to appreciate when you give them an ear.

Maintaining Focus During Conversations and Keeping People Interested

Once you start a conversation, the key is to keep it going and maintain interest. It's not always easy, and even people who are very comfortable in social situations may struggle with this. Not everyone is interesting to talk to, and not everyone appreciates certain topics of conversations. It's also not easy to know what people want to talk about, especially if you start the conversation with someone new. Meeting a new person is a fresh start and getting to know them means keeping them interested in you and what you have to say. There are some easy ways to do this, which may help keep people engaged:

Maintain eye contact, stay focused and avoid distractions. Eye contact should not be constant unless you notice that the person responds to it. Some people find continuous eye contact invasive and intimidating, while others find it engaging and a genuine show of interest. If someone talking to you looks away momentarily and/or only makes eye contact here and there, try doing the same. It will make them feel more comfortable.

Stay focused and indicate that you are interested in what they have to say. Nod, acknowledge, smile and making appropriate gestures and non-verbal cues can show that you are engaged and that the focus in one the conversation above all else. Avoiding distractions can mean moving to a quieter place and/or not looking away to see what other people are doing.

Ask open-ended questions that require a longer response than a simple "yes" or "no". If we do ask a question that responds with yes, or no, build on it. Ask more about their interest and/or reason(s) why. It's another way to learn about them and build a conversation around an interesting topic.

Listen carefully. Lending an ear is one of the best ways to stay engaged. If the other person enjoys communicating with you, this is a good sign that they are enjoying their interaction. They may also be nervous and talk a lot more because of it or want to make a good impression. We may find ourselves in a position where it's not just us, but the other person, who wants to maintain a good conversation and keep it going. In this scenario, good listening skills are the best option.

Techniques to Establish, Develop and Improve Self-Confidence

Self-confidence is easier to achieve for some and much more difficult for others. Improving how we see ourselves is key to improving our self-esteem and confidence. As covered in chapter one, taking an inventory of our positive attributes, skills and achievements are a significant part of this process. There are also some simpler, basic steps to take in order to get our focus or "inner voice" on the positive instead of focusing on our faults and weaknesses:

1.   Visualize yourself in a successful situation. It can be realistic or complete fantasy. Imagine that you are a superhero flying into disaster to rescue people or confronting a villain to stop them from doing harm. Whether it's a job or personal related feat of success, or a fantasy-fueled quest of bravery, put yourself in the starring role and become imaginative. When we see ourselves in an empowering, positive light, even for a few minutes, it can give us the boost of confidence we need to face certain situations. Even when there are no social scenarios to prepare for or challenges to face, this activity is enjoyable and can put us in a good mood. It also sets yourself up to "win".

2.   Eat well and take care of yourself. Do what you need to keep

healthy, fit and eating properly. When we feel stressed

and anxious, we may overeat or skip meals entirely. We may also neglect our health and become withdrawn. These are situations we should avoid at all costs. If you feel upset or impacted by a negative experience, go for a walk and drink lots of water.

Hydration and movement are helpful, basic ways to keep your mind focused. Remind yourself that you are important and deserving of good care and make self-care a priority. This can be very challenging if we are raising a family and/or have a demanding career, which makes time management a challenge.

Always make time for yourself, at least once a day, whether it's ten minutes on two hours. Taking care of your emotional, physical and mental health is of utmost importance.

3.   Affirmations are an excellent way to rid yourself of the negative thoughts and self-doubting that many of us have. We may underestimate the need for affirmations, but they can be very empowering and effective at building

our confidence. Affirmations are positive statements that are uplifting and encouraging. They counteract the negative comments that we internalize from other people, media and society in general. These positive statements need not be detailed or descriptive, but simple and direct: "You are valued."

"You are strong in body and mind." "You can do what you put your mind to."

Take a moment to reflect on what statements give you power or motivation. Is it something about your physical appearance that you want to embrace and accept, to feel more comfortable in your skin? "You are beautiful". If you want a better job and to make more income, "You are skilled and valuable." Don't underestimate the impact of simple statements. Affirmations are shared on social media often, alongside inspirational quotes and sayings. Take time to write your favorite affirmations down and decorate your washroom mirror or vanity with them. Make these statements visible; use other people's ideas or create your own.

44

4.   Take small risks. Skydiving or scaling a mountain may or may not be on your list of risks to take, so take a smaller risk or chance in life, and do it regularly. Try a new hairstyle or change your wardrobe. Visit another city or town you have never been to before. If traveling on your own is something you want to try, but have always felt afraid to do, take small trips by train, bus or a mini road trip. Keep a blog or journal about your trip and share your experience, or simply document for yourself. Learning a new sport, martial arts or scheduling a professional photoshoot are all ways to get outside of your comfort zone in a friendly, positive way.

5.   Be helpful to others. Sometimes engaging with other people or feeling good is a lot of work. It's a constant reminder of how fragile we can be, and yet we are strong and resilient too. Helping other people can be a powerful and wonderful way to realize that what we do has an impact on other people. Buying a coffee for someone down on their luck, volunteering at a shelter or

donating to a local charity are examples of how we can make a difference. It matters most that we are helping someone in need, and at the same time, we experience the joy of giving and making an impact in our community.

David Cooper

Chapter 2

READING BODY LANGUAGE

Understand Other People's Body Language and Using Our Own to Improve Communication

As we become more comfortable in mastering conversational skills and communicating effectively with other people, we'll notice a surge in confidence and an improved ability to feel comfortable in social situations. Learning to read and understand non-verbal cues and body language is equally important. While some people are good at communicating verbally exactly what is on their mind, not everyone will. Some people avoid disagreement or expressing their thoughts, but instead will convey their reactions in the form of gestures and other non-verbal movements.

48

A person's posture says a lot about their confidence. If a person keeps their back straight and looks ahead, they appear confident. If they slouch over, they may look intimidated or helpless. When this happens during a conversation, it can mean that either the person holds this posture regularly, if it is consistent, or has become very uncomfortable during the conversation if they suddenly slouch over and "hide". If this is the case, show some reassurance, or simply switch topics. Make the person feel comfortable.

Head motions, such as nodding, tilting to one side or another, are good signs. This indicates that the person is interested in you and what you have to say.

You are on the right track, keep it up!

The tapping of feet, fingers, or similar twitching or head movements can mean that someone is nervous or disturbed by something. They may not feel comfortable saying anything, but their body shows the signs of agitation, nervousness or impatience. If you notice any of these, slow down the conversation and try to engage more. Ask more about them and show interest. If this doesn't help, they may be distracted or not fully engaged in the first place. Some people may have other thoughts or worries on their mind, and not comfortable with discussing them. Simply remain patient and calm, and this may help their demeanor.

Hand gestures vary a lot and can mean many different things. Some people use their hands when they are enthusiastically describing something or telling a story, while other people may fidget or wring their hands when they are nervous while they talk. The use of hands during verbal and non-verbal communication can be cultural or simply a personal habit that has little or no bearing on the person's interest or communication. The folding of arms across the chest can signal a need to remain guarded or closed off somehow, while for other people, it's just comfortable.

Keeping a measure of distance is another way people communicate, by showing that they want to maintain a buffer zone or boundary with you. In these situations, the other person may be interested in what you have to say and actively engage verbally, while maintaining a strict distance. This can also be a sign of taking a defensive stance, particularly if the topic of conversation is emotionally charged or divisive in nature.

Non-Verbal Cues and Indicators of Communication

Watching for clues during a conversation can determine how someone is responding to us, which includes non-verbal gestures or motions. Some people may be quiet and unlikely to say how they honestly feel, and instead, fold their arms or distance themselves when they are unhappy. Other people may nod, smile and use hand gestures to indicate engagement. If we ignore how a person responds to our communicating with them, it can lead to misunderstanding and end a conversation. When we recognize how someone is reacting to us, taking action by adjusting how we correspond can make a big difference. In addition to body language and gestures, another way people communicate is how they dress or present themselves. If they dress formally to attend an event, even where formal attire is not required, they may want to make an impression with their appearance and style. For others, they simply prefer looking more professional and ready for business, maybe hoping for new business associates and connections at an event. For other people, the way they dress may be more casual, as a way to "blend in" or fit in with a crowd or group. Other people dress to make themselves appear more attractive or appealing, which they feel may improve their chances of meeting someone new.

Verbal sounds, such as "uh-huh" and "ummm" can convey certain emotions or thoughts, without actually putting those thoughts and ideas into words.

For example, "uh-huh" might be accompanied with a nod

or forward movement to show agreement and understanding, where "ummm" or other sounds of uncertainty or hesitation may signal disagreement or feelings of dismay. It's important to recognize these indicators right away, and respond by asking if a specific item is concerning or if the point of view is not mutual, taking a more proactive approach and keeping it civil, and moving onto another topic may be a better option:

"I understand politics/religion/news item (or another topic) is a bit of a hot topic, but it's a controversial one, maybe we could talk about _____ instead."

If someone is clearly upset to the point of not wanting to communicate any further, they may choose to vocalize at that point, or simply move away physically. One of the strongest non-verbal clues is using distance or other people, items as a way of creating a barricade or distance between you and them. It's a powerful statement and should be respected. We can do the same in situations that we may find offensive and difficult to respond to, choosing to leave the situation altogether. An example of how a person may distance themselves, apart from physically leaving a scene, may be sitting beside someone else, or leaving an empty chair between you and them, signaling a preference to maintain space.

Some people enjoy using props or objects when they tell a story or want to get every description. It has the effect of keeping other people's interests because it makes the conversation more interesting by keeping it visual.

Simple objects could be a wine glass, a napkin in a restaurant to use as a way to describe a scene in a story or experience, or using your body as a "prop" or visual to "act" out by posing, movement or making a facial expression for the purpose of getting a reaction. This can be very useful when using humor or drama and may be employed by very expressive, creative people looking to find others who relate to them in the same way.

All non-verbal cues are important to observe. One helpful exercise to try, the next time you are in a public space: observe people having a conversation and watch their body language. We don't have to know what they are saying or what the conversation is about, but merely observing how they react to one another. Are they nodding in agreement, tapping the other person on the shoulder or arm for reassurance, or are there arms folded, and do they appear withdrawn? There are many other expressions, movements, and poses that can provide a sign of how someone feels and learning to notice them will make communication much easier.

Improving Our Own Communication, Verbal and Non-Verbal for Positive Responses and Support

Once we become familiar with how to read and understand non-verbal forms of communication, we can learn to use them as well. Whether we realize it or not, people take notice of non-verbal cues and respond accordingly. Sometimes, when we don't feel comfortable to express ourselves verbally, and other times we simply don't know what words to use, so this is where gestures and body movements can convey what we want others to know and see.

In a group conversation, we may want to assert our voice so that we can be heard. Some of us have a loud voice, and a simple, but friendly word or two can get the attention you need. For other people, speaking up verbally makes them anxious, which is where gestures can be helpful. Raising your hand or smiling with a nod can get some people's attention. A quick wave of the hand can be a nice, and cheeky way of saying "I'm over here!" The demeanor of the crowd or group of people has everything to with how we respond and communicate, verbally or non-verbally. When we want to show confidence or give the appearance of being in control, we can sit or stand tall, with our back straight and head facing forward. Keeping our head raised, nodding and acknowledging others during conversation, is a good way to remain polite, engaged while exuding self- esteem. Turning to other people when the conversation moves to them, in a group setting, is a responsive and respectful way to show your commitment and engagement to what they have to say. It may also prompt them to communicate more with you, due to your show of interest. This is a good method to use in panel interviews because it shows that you are receptive, ready to adapt and have the confidence the achieve.

Nodding your head and smiling or adding appropriate facial expressions during a conversation is a lively and personal way to communicate. A person can say a lot with their facial expressions. There are obvious cues we make with our face that give away our feelings immediately, such as smiling or frowning, whereas raised eyebrows or a look of shock will show we are surprised or learning something unexpected. It's also a way to show the other person that you are interested in them and impacted by what they say. There are also more subtle ways to conveying interest and communicating with our face:

▫Use similar expressions to the person you are communicating with. This doesn't mean mimicking them, but rather keeping the facial signals subtle or minimal if they are subdued, or responding with stronger, but not too exaggerated, movements to keep them interested

▫Keep your face towards them, with your chin up and eyes focusing on them. This will indicate that you are paying attention and taking what they have to say seriously. When people feel that what they say isn't being heard, this action can make a significant difference.

▫Smile, but don't overdo it. Keep your gestures friendly and avoid over-exaggerating your facial expressions, as it may cause other people to see us as pretentious or inauthentic. It may also look as though we are trying to downplay or minimize a serious topic of conversation, or making others feel uncomfortable. When in doubt, tone down the expressions and gently smile.

The way we dress, project our image, and use our body, face, and the immediate area around us to express ourselves through non-verbal communication is powerful and can make a major impression, whether we have a verbal conversation or nod. We may simply notice a person sitting in an isolated setting, arms folded and head down, and know instantly that they are experiencing (or just experienced) a difficult situation where distance and "shutting down" was a means to escape an event. Other situations, where people make a point of staying within your view and making eye contact, can signal that they are interested in meeting you when they have the opportunity. Always take non-verbal cues seriously. In fact, they can be more honest and telling than what people actually mean to say, which is an advantage for us and how we respond to them.

David Cooper

CHAPTER 3
TIME MANAGEMENT

Practical Tips, Suggestions on Planning Your Schedule, and Managing Your Time Effectively to Reduce Stressful Situations

Everyone experiences stress. It is one of the most inevitable parts of life and there is often no way of avoiding it. There are methods to reduce the impact of stressful situations and curbing their impact on our life. One of the most effective methods is planning ahead with effective time management. Some people may consider time management when they organize their work schedule on a daily or weekly basis. It's also a way to plan family activities and itineraries for vacations and conferences.

Time management can also be an effective way to apply to our entire life's schedule so that we know exactly how to plan ahead...

Making a busy lifestyle and time constraints work in your favor: making the best use of a time schedule and reducing anxiety. Keeping a schedule up to date of appointments, work commitments, family events, and social breaks, is all part of a functioning schedule that can take the pressure off making us feel rushed or in a hurry. Managing time is just as important and valuable as managing money, as both take a lot of commitment and effort to earn, though are not always well spent or used. Consider your schedule or time management routine as a way to budget your life, and manage it with care, as you would your financial budget.

Schedule planning examples, charts, and ideas for time management

Time management is often overlooked and underestimated in its effectiveness. When we run late to a meeting or have to work harder to get a project done, it can be due to unforeseen circumstances that delay the process, or it can be a lack of management in the time we allocate to different jobs, tasks, and events in our life. Organizing a schedule can be as easy as using a calendar (monthly or weekly) to record how we plan to spend our time each day. We may already have commitments during most days, such as a full-time job from Monday through Friday, that limits the time we spend outside of work. When we consider how to budget our time, we can use a calendar with our schedule to combine an effective tool for time management. The example below provides an idea of what this type of schedule would look like:

Time management schedule sample 1: Monday through Friday

Time frame	Monday	Tuesday	Wednesday	Thursday	Friday
6-7 am	Exercise (jogging)	Exercise (cycling)	Yoga	Exercise (jogging)	Exercise (cycling)
7-8 am	Get ready for work, eat breakfast	Get ready for work, eat breakfast	Get ready for work, eat breakfast	Get ready for work, eat breakfast	Get ready for work, eat breakfast

8-9 am	Commute to work	Dentist appointment until 10 am	Commute to work	Commute to work	Commut to work
9 am – 12 pm	Work	Work	Conference call 11-12 pm	Work	Work
12-1 pm	Lunch	Lunch	Lunch	Lunch	Lunch
1-5 pm	Work	Work	Work	Work	Work
5-6 pm	Commute home	Commute home	Commute home	Commute home	Commut home
9-7:30 pm	Dinner	Dinner	Take out for dinner	Dinner	Dinner
7:30 - 9 pm	Read	Read/study for an exam	Read	Dance class	Dinner with friends

9-10pm	Sleep	Reading, sleep	Sleep	Late night snack/reading	Sleep
10-11 pm	Sleep	Sleep	Sleep	Sleep	Sleep

The schedule above is an example of a standard week of a full-time work week with a few changes: a dentist appointment on Tuesday, a conference call on Wednesday a social evening on Friday. The majority of the schedule is fairly common and uneventful, which is expected. For a busy schedule that includes weekends as either part of the workweek or included with other events that need to be managed to ensure there is enough time and to determine how long each activity will take to complete.

The next schedule is more flexible, in that it involves a work-from-home schedule with weekends. A more fluid time frame can make scheduling easier, though when work occurs at different times each day, there is a lack of consistency. This may work well for some people, and not so much for others.

When we get used to a nine-to-five style schedule, or a similar version of it, moving to a more flexible schedule can result in some unwanted changes in our behavior and habits, including:

▣Procrastination. When a schedule is more flexible and the hours are determined by us, then we might take advantage of this feature and delay some projects in favor of more time to ourselves.

▣Inconsistency. We may not get us much done unless we use more self-discipline. This is where time management is important and can essentially "force" us to work at certain intervals and within certain blocks of time.

Avoiding unwanted results, whether are schedules are routine or more flexible, can give us a lot more consistency in how we approach new tasks and events. In the more flexible, work-at-home schedule, all seven days are included, as work can be shifted to a weekend if needed, to make room for appointments, family commitments, and social engagements. Making time for every aspect of our life is important for success and understanding how long to "budget" or allocate for each event is equally important. For example, if we know that a dentist's appointment will take more than an hour, budget two hours instead of one or one and a half. The "extra" half- hour will allow for some flexibility, especially when traffic is heavy or other delays may occur. We may also be required to wait longer than expected for certain events. Some scheduled items, such as classes or exercise routines, are predictable and can be easily manageable, though working on an ongoing project or taking a road trip can vary widely depending on changing conditions: more research needed for a project or taking a detour on the way home from a day trip.

Time management schedule sample 2: Monday through Sunday (full 7-day week)

Time frame	Monday	Tuesday	Wednesday	Thursday	Friday
6-7 am	Exercise (jogging)	Exercise (cycling)	Yoga	Exercise (jogging)	Exercise (cycling)
7-8 am	Get kids ready for school, make lunches	Get kids ready for school, make lunches	Get kids ready for school, make lunches	Get kids ready for school, make lunches	Get kids ready for school, make lunches
8-9 am	Enjoy breakfast, read the news	Work on project 2	Meet a new client, go to the spa for the morning	Work on project 3	Prepare and take the exam at a local college
9 am – 12 pm	Work on project 1				
12-1 pm	Lunch		Lunch	Meet with one of the	Lunch
1-2 pm	Lunch	Go cycling,	Doctor's appointment	kids' teachers	Arrive home on work

2-6 pm	Work on project 1 (pick up kids from	pick up kids from school	Work on project 2	Lunch, and continuing to work on project 3	more on project 3
6-7:30 pm	school)	Dinner	Order dinner for delivery	Dinner	Dinner
7:30-9 pm	Dinner	Read/study for an exam (online course)	Go to the theater, enjoy a late-night snack	Read/study for an exam tomorrow	Enjoy a live concert
9-10pm	Start on project 2		Sleep		
10-11 pm	Sleep	Sleep			
11 pm	Sleep	Sleep	Sleep	Sleep	

There are helpful tips to consider when preparing a time management chart or schedule. These steps can provide a way to approach how we value and prioritize all of the tasks and items in our life:

1.   Make a list of all the things you do. This may seem like a daunting task, especially if you find yourself

constantly busy, from working full-time to raising a family and/or working on various projects and running common errands and chores. It's important to include everything, even the items you don't perform other, but at least weekly.

2. When the list is complete, post it on your refrigerator or desk, so that it is readily available to review and add more items if necessary. This is the initial phase of planning your time management. You may already have a calendar for organizing your schedule, and this is the next step.

3. Rearrange your list to prioritize from the most important to the least important. The first items on your list may be making important commitments with family or work, as well as medical appointments. This will change from week to week, and for this reason, adjust your list to expand the frequency of each commitment.

4.   When prioritizing items on your list, remember these will be the events that will go on your time management schedule first, followed by another, a second layer of priority. This effect of layering will ensure that your most important items are scheduled first, before anything else.

5.   For some of us, the list becomes full fast, and it can be a daunting task to schedule everything. In this case, try finding some items that can be omitted or moved to a later time or the following week. Trying a new restaurant or taking the kids to a new theme park are important for our well-being, though they are adjustable events that can be rescheduled or shifted as needed.

6.   Delegate as much as possible. Find people to help you where it's needed. Sometimes we think we have to do everything on our own, and when we do, it becomes more stressful and exhausted. At the end of a stressful, draining week, we may not feel like socializing at all or have the

energy to do anything else. Delegating chores to family or asking co-workers for help is a good way to lightening your plate and making the weekly grind easier.

7.   Take care of yourself and schedule "me" time. As much as our job, family and friends need us and we need them, we also need that alone time to recharge and simply do nothing. Even one hour of solitude can work wonders, giving us a sense of slowing down the fast pace of life and taking much needed time to relax and feel human again.

8.   Plan ahead. Preparing a time management schedule from week to week or for the next month is important, but it's also important to take time to plan further ahead for vacations, large scale projects, and family commitments. This can alleviate a lot of last-minute preparation and aggravation that can be avoided when we have as much planned in advance as possible.

9.	Avoid distractions and make a point of finding a space or environment, as much as possible, to get work done. This can be difficult in situations where we are constantly around people who keep us distracted and busy. Becoming less distracted can be a developed skill using meditation and taking more breaks to recharge and refocus.

10.Accept that not everything can be done as planned. When we accept this, it becomes easier to go with the flow of certain situations that inevitably change, whether we want them to or not. This can mean politely saying "no" when we are used to always agreeing and following along. It's important to establish that boundary so that other people understand that we have our limits, as everyone does.

David Cooper

CHAPTER 4

UNDERSTAND EMOTIONS

AND PERSONALITIES

Variations in Emotional Responses to Situations and Scenarios in Life

How we respond in various situations can make a significant difference in the outcome and the way we communicate with others. Emotional responses are especially delicate, as people are not always keen on sharing their emotions. Some feelings are either hidden or expressed much differently than expected. When we are faced with a crisis, we either fight, flight or freeze (shut down).

This is based on the "fight or flight" method, which indicates one of two responses will occur when we are faced with an immediately dangerous or traumatic situation: we either "fight", meaning we stand up and take charge right away, either to defend our self or someone else, or we proceed with the "flight" open, where we rung away to avoid serious harm or consequence. Depending on the specific circumstance, it is difficult to determine which is most often used. In a situation where social anxiety occurs, a person may choose the "flight" option, effectively leaving a party, conference or social event to avoid interacting with other people.

When choosing the "fight" option in this instance, the opposite occurs: the person remains at the event or within the group and makes an effort to communicate. The "freeze" option is when neither flight or fight occurs, and the person simply stays but does not engage with anyone. How do people typically react in life-threatening situations? They will often use the least dangerous option or one that is based on survival mode...

The Proactive Approach Versus Reactive

We all react to unexpected surprises or challenging situations. We might react verbally, expressing our distaste, or shock. In some scenarios, we see a situation occur that cannot be anticipated. In many cases, we can often predict the outcome of an event by our familiarity with the people involved and circumstances. For example, we may know someone will become aggressive when a certain topic is discussed, or if they encounter a particular individual or debate. It's not always easy to prevent a challenging interaction with other people, though it can be done in many circumstances.

Proactive and reactive are terms that mean reacting before or after an incident. When we take a proactive approach, we try to minimize or prevent something that may cause a problem later. If you notice signs of tension during a conversation or the potential for an explosive argument between people, you may take action before it happens, by setting certain controls in place. This can be done by explaining a situation empathetically before delivering bad news, for example. When steps are taken to control or minimize the possible negative outcome of a situation, it is preventative in nature and can save us a lot of grief by avoiding inevitable reactions.

When taking the reactive approach, it is the exact opposite of proactive. We become reactive or react to an event after it has occurred, either because we were not able to prevent it from happening or chose not to do so. The reactive option is basically damage control and can be effective, though more limiting than proactive.

Proactive Versus Reactive Scenario:
Anniversary Party

There is a small anniversary party organized for a group of twenty people. Most of the people are close family, with a few friends, and while they are all fond of the couple celebrating their tenth wedding anniversary, among this group of people is a separated pair, Angela and Dan, who have not spoken in six months.

Fortunately for the married couple, they have managed to remain close friends with both Angela and Dan separately, and are sensitive to both sides of the reasons for their split. On the surface, the separation appears amicable, and both Dan and Angela individually assure their hosts that they are more than accepting of the other's attendance at the event.

The invitations are sent out, and Dan responds that he will attend, asking if he can bring his new girlfriend Sam. The hosting couple is shocked, but agree to it, as they value their friendship with Dan. Angela, on the other hand, is hoping to reconcile in the future with Dan, though doesn't expect it to happen anytime soon. She would also like to attend and sends her confirmation.

In considering the types of personalities both Dan and Angela have, the host couple knows they are prone to explosive arguments, and on at least one previous occasion, things got physical. They want to avoid any chance of this happening and know they need to take action, one way or another to avoid a disaster. They discuss the situation prior to the anniversary party and come up with the options:

<u>Option 1:</u>
The host couple decide to contact Angela and explain that Dan has indicated he plans to attend with a date. Angela becomes emotional and angry, not only because Dan is bringing his date, but also because the couple didn't

object to it. She decides not to attend and sternly explains that her friendship with the couple is at risk and feels that they don't value her in their lives. On the evening of the party, Dan attends with his date Sam, introducing her to the host couple. They are pleased with Sam, though disappointed in Dan for what they consider an insensitive decision to date so soon after breaking up with Angela. The party goes well, but their friendship with Angela is effectively done, and they become distant with Dan, not inviting him to any further events.

Option 2:

The host couple decide to allow Dan to bring his date, Sam, though they do not inform Angela, hoping the situation will remain civil when they all arrive, considering there are others at the party, and they will engage with them in conversation, keeping them distracting from each other. They consider encouraging Angela to invite a guest of her own, though she declines, preferring to attend solo. The offer does make her suspicious and nervous, and on the night of the party, her concerns are verified when she notices Dan with his new date. It causes a loud outburst, followed by a screaming match between Dan and Angela, across a room full of festive people. This dampens everyone's mood, including Sam, Dan's date, who was under the impression that Dan was already divorced or at least separated for a few years. Most people decide to leave the party shortly after, thanking the couple for the invite, but eager to depart. The couple tries to liven up the atmosphere with a round of drinks and some music, but the damage is done. It leaves a negative impression on everyone.

Option 3:

The host couple decide to meet with Dan separately when he asks to bring his date. They meet for lunch and ask about Dan's new girlfriend. He's thrilled to bring her to the party, but the couple explain that doing this will be off- putting to Angela, with whom they also want to invite. They explain to Dan that they value their friendship with both of them, and in doing so, would prefer Dan not bring Sam, until a later occasion, when Angela has moved on or is ready to find out about her. Dan disagrees. He's visibly upset, but his reaction is more disappointed than angry. He agrees to attend without Sam. Angela is made aware that Dan has a girlfriend, but that he does not intend to bring her. She is grateful to the host couple for letting her know and politely asking Dan to hold off on bringing Sam. They both attend and the party goes well. Dan leaves early to see Sam, and Angela stays after the party to help clean up.

All three options to scenario 1 illustrate how proactive and reactive approaches work. In option 1, the approach is somewhat proactive, in that the couple gives Angela a "heads up" on her estranged husband's new girlfriend, though they do nothing further to quell the tension or address Dan's decision to bring her. For this reason, they risk losing their friendship with Angela. In option 2, the couple uses a reactive approach, taking no preventative measures, and instead, hoping there is no confrontation between the estranged couple. This goes horribly wrong, and in the end, does not fare well for anyone in attendance. The final option 3 is more proactive because both Dan and Angela are approached separately and in a non-threatening or non-confrontational manner. The couple's decision to take the time to prepare their two guests for the party is not necessary but goes along with to prevent an explosive situation.

In reality, there is no guarantee that a proactive or reactive approach will work best, though proactive is usually the best option because it aims to create an environment in which the most positive outcome will result. The proactive way of handling a situation takes more effort, work and sometimes it can be initially more stressful, though a much better chance of a decent outcome with less anxiety and damage is a goal to strive for.

Tips for Understanding Emotions and Different Personalities

How People Express Emotions Differently

When we experience an emotion or communicate with other people who react emotionally, this varies from one individual to the next. We may not all react or express ourselves in the same way, even if we feel the same or similar emotion. Understanding how people feel versus express how they feel can help us better handle conversations and communication with different people. Often, the way we express or suppress how we feel is rooted in how we are raised, cultural and societal norms and sometimes it's an individual choice.

In some cultures, the expression of emotion is embraced and accepted. People brought up in an environment that doesn't shame or stop others from showing emotions, such as grief, anger or disappointment, as examples are beneficial in that people can release those feelings without fear of being seen as "weak" or unable to control their feelings. It's completely normal to show or display emotions, as long as our behavior does not become dangerous or harmful, such as becoming physically violent when experiencing anger, or becoming harmful to another person because of jealousy or grief.

For some people and cultures, suppressing certain emotions is expected, and any sign of sadness, fear or anger is frowned upon. This can have a negative effect on some people who need to find an outlet for their feelings, especially after experiencing a loss. In certain ways of upbringing and societies, showing happiness and agreement are expected constantly, and any sign of disagreement is discouraged, even stigmatized. This is problematic for people who need to fulfill the need to communicate honestly and authentically. When we are expected to act "happy" all the time, we may be coerced, even subtly, that any feelings less than contentment signal a problem with our selves instead of treating the emotion as a normal part of life. Individually, everyone has their own way of expressing how they feel. Some people who are open about showing how they feel may be called "dramatic" or "over-dramatic" to those who choose a more subdued or low-profile way of expression. When we experience a loss or event that causes sadness and grieving, there are different stages that each of us will go through as we process the event and learn to adapt, while suffering from the loss. Some people may openly talk about the effect of the loss; the death of a loved family member or friend, losing a pet or being diagnosed with a serious health condition. Studies conducted on the effects of grief and loss indicate talking and sharing experiences one-on-one or in a group setting are very helpful for coping. For other people, they may move through the stages of grieving quietly, and choose not to discuss their feelings with anyone. Social anxiety can play a role in how we choose to express our emotions, though the most important aspect of dealing with any situation that is emotionally charging is to get the support and coping skills needed to help you at the moment, and in the long-term.

Understanding Different Personality Types

Personality types and differences vary considerably, and we often notice this at work, in groups settings and even within our own family. Understanding the basic types of personalities and how they affect us is important in knowing how to respond and communicate effectively. Some people value a strong, direct vocal response, while others prefer a more quiet, careful and diplomatic approach. Sometimes, the personality can incorporate different moods and changes in one person, making conversation difficult and sometimes unpredictable. Learning how to recognize general characteristics and what they look like can help us understand and communicate more effectively.

When we consider the people in our immediate social and professional circle, we may see them in one way or another. For example, most people are either categorized as an extrovert or an introvert. People described as extroverts are defined as very outgoing, social and skilled at networking and starting conversations. They are the "life of the party" and tend to ignite a spark in social gatherings. Extroverts tend to do well in sales, high-profile careers that deal with the public and jobs that require good liaising with others. They also tend to be uninhibited and do not hesitate in social situations as other people might. Extroverts will take risks and people tend to find them appealing, friendly and energetic. Some people who exhibit an extroverted personality can be seen as arrogant and too confident. This can hinder their progress, where a more modest or calm approach is desired.

Introverts, on the other hand, are the opposite of extroverts. People described as introverted tend to be low-key, quiet and avoid social situations. In fact, people who experience social anxiety may be considered introverted, for their avoidance of social situations. Introverts are characterized as shy, self- focused and tend to internalize their feelings and emotions. Communication with someone described as introverted can be challenging if they are very withdrawn and hesitant to respond. They tend to listen to their inner voice more and focus on their innermost thoughts and feelings without expressing them. Realistically, most people fall somewhere between extrovert and introvert. Some people who keep to themselves may be considered introverted in certain groups or situations, though may openly socialize more in other groups. Extroverts may communicate less in certain scenarios where they may not feel comfortable or lack confidence, even when they appear over-confident.

The way we express ourselves can mask how we genuinely feel, depending on the situation. It can be used as a defense mechanism when we feel the need to take caution around certain people. We may behave more quietly around people who gossip or talk excessively and feel more relaxed and conversational in a different climate altogether. There are people who consider themselves ambiverts, which incorporates attributes of both introverts and extroverts. The way they behave can depend a lot on their mood, surroundings and/or how people communicate with them.

General Personality Types in Everyday Life

We may not consider what type of personality type we have, or others have until it's asked in a job interview or we find ourselves in conflict with someone who clashes with our own personality. The following types of personalities are generalizations, though they can describe the characteristics of certain people, why they behave a certain way and how to communicate with them:

Nurturing/Parental Personalities:

This personality describes a caring person, who may have strong values and principles about supporting and helping others. Nurses, caregivers, social workers, and certain types of advocates for marginalized people can easily fit into this category. Most nurturing and caring people are consistently this way and usually reserve judgment, often looking after people who are vulnerable or disadvantaged in one way or another.

Empaths:

People with a strong sense of empathy towards others are very sensitive to their own emotions and the feelings of others. These sensations can be strong at times, and it gives them the ability to connect and empathize with the way other people feel. They are genuine in their connection, and similar in some ways, to the nurturing/parental personality type. They are different in that they rely on intuition and emotion and may not always use the most practical approach when handling certain situations.

"Pioneer" or Dominant Personalities:

These people are considered bold, upfront, and sometimes very blunt and direct. They tend to dominate conversations and focus on goals. They are usually ambitious and focused on the future, sometimes possessing strategic skills for planning, though may be rigid and restrictive. Dominant personalities can be exhausting, as they allow little or no room for others' opinions or input unless it benefits their goals.

Protectors:

People who take ownership and responsibility for themselves and sometimes others' actions are seen as protectors. They tend to be practical, sensible and fair, sometimes taking on more than they should. Protectors can also be logical and clear-headed, remaining calm in difficult situations and helping others cope.

Creative Personalities:

They are visionaries and are creative with their ideas and solutions. They usually envision the big picture and how the pieces of everything fits together, where others focus on specific areas or details.

There are other personality traits in addition to these five, including combinations of two or more. For example, a person with a nurturing, parental personality type may also be a protector, whereas a dominant person may be creative, using their creative skills to achieve goals and stay one step ahead. How do these different personalities impact our communication with people? In our everyday life, we have been in contact with many different types of people and their personalities. How we converse with them makes a major impact on whether the communication is effective or not, how we are interpreted and taken seriously.

Communication with Different Personality Types

People with strong personalities will always be a challenge. The dominant or "pioneer" personality is one of the most difficult, in that a person fitting this role will want to take the lead and delegate, rather than listen. They may be considered a "pioneer" if they want to blaze a new path or direction in a company and be noticed as a founder of a project or business venture. When approaching someone in this role, taking a subdued yet firm voice is usually effective. A dominant person or someone striving for dominance will respond well to someone who appears to be an asset in their plan, or who may be able to assist them in one way or another. For example, instead of saying: "I have a great idea that may help you with___", which may be seen as

challenging their position of authority or perceived sense of power. Instead, approach them gently, mentioning that you are interested in what they are working on and that you would like to be of assistance where possible. It may not be the way you want to convey yourself, but it will get your message across more effectively if they view you as someone humbly looking to help, rather than taking over (as they may perceive it this way).

Creative people can be engaging and enthusiastic when they feel strongly about a vision and will respond well to communication that supports their way of thinking and views of the world. Creative personalities tend to be idealistic and fun, though not always practical. When communicating with them on a topic, you may notice that they become drawn to the big picture and large-scale ideas and thoughts. It can be both interesting and sometimes tricky to navigate through a conversation with them, when they are enjoying listening to themselves describe a new concept or plan. In this way, they are similar to a dominant personality type, where their ego and project take center stage, and everything must follow. In communicating with them, listen first, to get an idea of where their interests lie. If they are passionate about food or music, for example, ask them about their tastes and a recommendation. This will give them a chance to focus on your questions, with an opportunity to discuss more.

Protectors and nurturing personality types are easier to converse with than other personalities. Their moods tend to be stable and they are clear-headed, focused and consistent. Once they make a decision, they usually stick with the plan and will not change unless there is a logical reason to do so. People who aim to protect are also good at self-improvement and taking/accepting responsibility for their actions. They respond well to constructive criticism and actually respect someone who speaks up and takes charge. A nurturing personality is also protective, acting as a mentor for others. In management or parental role, they can be invaluable as a resource or support system for many people, without passing judgment. They are good listeners and have good intentions. They are approachable, so whether you are quiet and reserved or wish to be bold in your communication, they are equipped to handle both and accepting of many different people and their own personalities.

People with an empath-type of personality are usually sensitive and keen to others' feelings and emotions. They may respond well to your way of communication if you approach them carefully and with a calm demeanor. In some situations, depending on the type of conversation or items discussed, an empath may become emotional or passionate in expressing their thoughts and feelings about a certain topic or social issue. A good example of this

David Cooper

would be someone who feels strongly about a vegan lifestyle with no tolerance for the use of animal products. While some people can argue for a vegan lifestyle based on the science and health benefits of it, an empath will use the emotional side of the discussion to provoke empathy from others. When other people simply do not respond in kind, an empath may be deeply affected by what they consider an insensitive or rude response from someone, even if it is perceived by others as logical and reasonable. When communicating with an empath, thread carefully, using your own emotions or feelings as part of the conversation, such as "I understand what you mean. I feel that____" or "I feel strongly that_____" By inserting your own sense of feeling or "passion" into the conversation, an empath may be able to identify with you and discussion will be smooth and easy.

Personalities, moods, and emotions vary widely and identifying certain attributes early in other people can make communication with them effective and easier. In effect, we are using a form of diplomacy by assessing another person's demeanor and personality before we engage. This is always a good way to minimize misunderstanding while increasing the potential for good relations and conversation.

CHAPTER 5
IMPROVING YOUR
COMMUNICATION SKILLS

Creating a Friendlier, Amicable Environment for Better Communication within a Challenging One

Improving your communication skills is more than focusing on you, as it includes knowing the environment your life and work in as well. This can be a daunting task when we must face stressful and challenging situations daily. A high-stress environment can create anxiety, and when this happens, we may prefer to turn inward and avoid social contact as much as possible. When we do communicate is an unstable or stressful place, we may express agitation, frustration or indifference. We may see our space as hopeless and at times, impossible to deal with, not to mention communicate in. Sometimes we can change where we are, and this may work in many situations until we find our self in a new challenging place. For other people, changing locations or avoiding certain people is not possible, and we are simply expected to face situations that are not the easiest to deal with.

One example of a difficult situation may be an abusive or toxic person in our life. They may not be physically violent, though use their words to emotionally and verbally mistreat others. This can take a toll on our self-confidence and how others may see us. Other difficult situations may include working with people who can be demanding and unreasonable, regardless of our efforts, making us feel inadequate about our self-worth and performance.

The following options may be considered when handling very challenging environments and/or people:

Avoid difficult people and situations as much as possible, whenever and however you can. If they are difficult because of abusive behavior, you may require support from your employer or a someone in a professional capacity (therapist, counselor) that can give you more specific guidance on how to remove yourself (and others, such as family, co-workers) from abusive situations. When we are unable to avoid or leave a difficult situation, consider that the situation is temporary and remain calm as much as possible. Keep your responses minimal with people who are rude or insulting. If you need to speak up, keep your words firm, but calm. Be loud enough to be heard and let them know that their mistreatment will not be tolerated.

Every day has its potential to get better or worse, and keeping a healthy, positive mindset is the best way to begin. Use daily affirmations as a way to boost your self-confidence and know that you are worth being treated with respect and dignity. Always keep this in mind.

One of the triggers for a verbal attack occurs when someone feels as though they are treated unfairly. They may blame you for their misfortune and make a scene in front of you and/or others.

Remain calm and address them in this way: explain that you had no intention of any mistreatment or unfairness and ask what they need. It doesn't matter if you are at fault or not, or whether you need to fix the problem. It is a way to help them recognize why they are angry. This usually gives the other person a chance to pause and consider what they want out of it. Some people get so involved with their anger or frustration, that they no longer think about resolving the issue, but just expressing the anger. Giving them the chance to help solve the problem causing their reaction is empowering to them and gives you a chance to figure out what the root of their problem is.

Not every challenging situation is the same. Some

scenarios are toxic and abusive that leaving is the only real option, while other situations can be resolved with a careful, calm demeanor with non-intimidating words and language. The most important way to approach an angry or potentially explosive situation is to not engage in the same manner. As tempting as it may be to shout or yell back, especially if we are hurt or feel angry (even justifiably) in response, it will only escalate the situation more, and there could be reprisal and possible violence if a person feels challenged. Even if your response in anger or frustration is a justified response, avoid a disaster and try to calm the situation before leaving the room or area altogether.

Sometimes when we face difficult situations, we feel alone and unsupported. This is usually an exaggerated reaction to the way we see our self sometimes, especially if we often do things alone or do not feel comfortable asking for help. It's always good to consider that a lot of people will step up and help, even during a challenging scenario. Sometimes others observe and understand what we are going through, even if we are not aware. If there is someone you feel comfortable talking to about difficult situations at home or work, this can be an invaluable means of support. You can also be the same support to someone else; if confronting a person "attacking" you or another person is not safe nor comfortable, stand with the other person instead. Let them know you can help them get what they need and will stay with them until the situation is safe.

Practical Exercises and Methods to use to Create Brilliant, Intelligent Conversations

When we start a conversation, whether we are meeting someone for the first time, or getting reacquainted with someone we already know or have met before, we usually start with small talk. It's a practical, easy way to break the ice and it makes communication more comfortable. Once we break through the initial chatter, it can get boring fast.

This is where switching to an intelligent conversation is the goal of really getting to learn about someone, their interests, while making a good impression of yourself on them and others. A good first impression and greeting are important, but what follows is even more impactful.

What are the benefits of having deep, brilliant conversations? They are more satisfying and make us think more critically. Sometimes, the person we converse with might be helpful and interesting ideas that are enjoyable to discuss. People who enjoy deeper conversations tend to be happier and experience more satisfaction in their social life. They may not be keen on a small talk at all, using it only to get things started, and once the discussion gets more interesting, a common bond can develop that may be more meaningful. Meeting the same person or people again in the future will pay off, as they will remember you for you good conversation and knowledge, not just small talk.

How can you transition from small talk to an intelligent, meaningful conversation? It can be an easy process with some people, and a bit more involving with others. If the other person is keen on starting the conversation or moving into a more in-depth topic, the best practice at that point is to simply listen and acknowledge. It may be a topic you are familiar with, or something completely new. Either way, it's an opportunity to make an impression:

If you know about the topic, then engagement is easy. You'll pick up on the flow of the conversation easily and feel confident because of the knowledge you already have. In the event you do not have any ideas or previous knowledge of the topic, ask questions. Listening and asking questions are two basic ways to stay engaged with someone while learning from what they have to say. They may have a lot to say on a specific item, or their expertise in a certain profession can give you insight into something new and interesting. If they notice your interest in conversing with them, a person will stay engaged in conversation for a long time. Here are some key techniques to try when beginning (or engaging in) an intelligent conversation:

1.   Ask the right questions and use good judgment. People love attention and asking them about a topic that they are familiar with will prompt them to talk more, while giving you valuable information at the same time. Try asking questions at the right time, when there is a pause in the conversation. Rephrase certain information to show you are paying attention; by doing this, you'll also become more knowledgeable about the topic being discussed.

2.   Try a new approach. When people ask how you are, we usually answer with "I'm fine" or "I'm good, and how are you?" Instead,
we can make a unique statement or impression by saying something like: "I'm ready for an adventure or a vacation" or "I'm looking forward to reading (mention a

specific book)". This type of response will unexpectedly start an interesting, and fun conversation. It also gives the other person the impression that there's more to you than a generic response to a greeting.

3.　　Think of an interesting story to share. It doesn't have to be too personal or your story. It could be a fact discovered while touring a historic site on a vacation or discovering a new fencing club in your neighborhood. It doesn't have to be a dramatic event. In fact, keep it light-hearted, fun and fascinating. This is a great way to create a link from small talk to a more interesting discussion.

4.　　Avoid cookie-cutter responses and jump into a new direction with something more thrill-seeking. Instead of asking how much they are enjoying the weather, ask about the most daring rollercoaster they enjoy or mention an unusual bucket list item that you are considering checking "done" soon. Think of slightly personal, bizarre and fun items as a way to procure a good conversation.

5.   Discuss a project that you are working on. This can be anything from painting a picture, renovating a room in your home or starting a new blog. Sharing your creative side is a way to make a conversation interesting without getting too personal. Think of your journey to deciding on a specific project or goal. If you started a new blog, for example, about exotic plants or bizarre historical facts, this is definitely worth sharing and discussing.

6.   Focus on the other person. Everyone has something about them that is unique and interesting. Make it a goal to find out what that uniqueness is in other people. They will find your approach personable and fun, without feeling invasive or probing. You can simply ask: "If you have to think of something unique or bizarre about yourself, what would it be?" It's not a personal question, as much as it is a focus on finding someone's creativity. Starting an intelligent or brilliant conversation doesn't require a degree or reading numerous books on specific topics to impress other people. Most people are content to

keep conversation light, even when a deeper topic is broached, humor and using your imagination is almost always welcome. Keep in mind that in social circles, people tend to unwind, which means discussing a deep topic be not be approached formally, but usually as a byproduct of a more fun topic or story.

Discover Your Own Potential and Hidden Talents that You Have

When we think of talents, we may imagine a television show where contestants compete for the spotlight or an opportunity to perform before millions. We may associate talent with specific people we know in life, and skills they have, such as playing a guitar or piano proficiency or speaking several languages fluently. Sometimes we don't realize that talents are not always obvious. There are many hidden talents that we possess that can boost our confidence, once we discover them. Sometimes talents are discovered naturally in childhood when we learn to play an instrument or sing. We may be good with strategy, which makes a good candidate for chess. These are examples of skills and talents that we become aware of and practice to improve our ability. There are also many hidden talents that can be discovered with the right guidance, though we may not consider looking for them. Here are a few ways to search within ourselves for skills, talents and unique characteristics that we may not realize we have:

Take a look into your past, into your childhood, and various stages throughout your life. Were there any hobbies or enjoyable activities that you practiced then that you may be good at now?

For example, we might have enjoyed painting or sketching, without realizing the potential of developing our skills later on in life. Do you remember anyone telling you how good you were at doing certain things? For some people, they may have been told they were good with animals or good at making people laugh. A good sense of humor is a great way to communicate, and a talent that many people may not realize they have.

_What do you enjoy? Write down everything you like to do or would like to try. Begin with the things you're familiar with first, then decide if there is something worth pursuing. If an old hobby comes to mind, make time to engage in it again. Hobbies can be the source of happiness that we need in our life to increase our confidence, whether we think we are good at it or not. It's a source of stress relief and reduces anxiety. It can also be improved upon and become a true talent.

_Were you ever recognized for an accomplishment or skill? This can be as simple as getting recognized for your hard work and dedication on the job, to being rewarded in grade school for your knowledge of science or an A+ on an essay or writing project.

116

Focus on what people recognize you for. This can lead to hidden talents and abilities beyond what we think. For example, a high grade in history may not make us a historian, but it can indicate a good memory for learning and memorizing dates, events, and key historical figures.

Once you list the hobbies and things you like to do, rate how good you are at them. Be honest, but not too hard on yourself. We might enjoy a game of bowling, though may not be the highest score, though we may be good at playing billiards or darts. Try a few local places where you can practice a skill or hobby to improve and decide if it's a worthwhile pursuit. The key is to enjoy what you do.

This idea may be lengthy, though it may be worthwhile to write your story. It doesn't have to be detailed, or thorough, but it can be the interesting experiences in your life that made an impact: the people, places, and experiences that shape who we are. Within these stories

117

may lie some interests that translate into a talent or two.

Try something new. Take a risk and move outside of your comfort zone. It doesn't have to be a risky sport or life-altering event. Attending an art class and meeting new people may be a good way to try a new hobby and find out if a skill can emerge from it. Learning a new form of dance or training for a marathon are other examples of developing skills for new talents.

Make a point of trying something new often, or at least once every two or three months. If possible, visit a new place or try a new hobby once a month. It's natural to feel nervous or unsure of trying something new at first, though once you jump into the new experience, you'll find it gets easier, as well as enjoyable. When you join or take a new class, there is also the potential to meet like-minded people with similar hobbies and talents.

David Cooper

CHAPTER 6

DEALING WITH DIFFICULT PEOPLE

Identifying and Recognizing the Signs of a Toxic Relationship

When we improve our self-confidence by setting positive goals, taking care of ourselves and improving our ability to communicate and reduce social anxiety, we will meet new people. Getting familiar with new people can lead to friendship and in some cases, the start of a new relationship. Other connections can lead to stronger networking at work and in our community. As we get to know people, we will come across toxic personalities that can hinder a lot in our life. Just when we start to improve in many areas and begin to thrive, there are some people who wish to make other people their target for

120

manipulation and malice. These are considered toxic people, and they should be avoided at all costs. Toxic people are not always obvious. They are usually friendly, approachable and seem like the life of the party. They may have an intense personality and know how to keep us interested. There are traits and characteristics that will help you identify which people are toxic early in your relationship with them:

Instantly Falling in Love

If someone you've just met thinks you are the love of your life, it's a good sign to break away then and there. "Falling" for someone can happen when we are attracted to them physically, which can happen quickly, though it does not mean we truly love or care for them. Real love and fondness for someone develop over a period of time, as you get to know them and who they really are. We may initially enjoy their company and want to be a relationship, only to find out later that their personality traits and attitude do not match our own. For this reason, anyone trying to convince you in "love at first sight" if simply trying to play games. Don't be fooled!

They take over your life

It's normal to have a social life with family and friends. Even if we are not the most social, we still need time for ourselves to break and enjoy

life in solitude or with other people. When we begin a relationship with someone, we tend to increase the time we spend with them, and this makes sense since we are getting to know them and want to develop things further. When your partner or friend becomes possessive or tries to limit your time outside of their being with you, it's a red flag. If you end up canceling plans with your best friend or skip a few lunch dates with co-workers or friends, because your new partner may want you to themselves, it's not a healthy situation. It's a form of isolation to keep you with them more than anyone else.

They want to control more and more of your life, by limiting not only your social interaction with other people but on your own as well.

Feeling Emotionally Drained

A relationship is a commitment and can take a lot of effort. While this is normal, the effort should come from both partners. When it becomes one-sided, where you do all the changing, giving and accommodating to please your partner, even at the detriment of friendships and family, and they do nothing or little in return, it's definitely becoming a toxic situation, and not worth doing all the work for little in return.

Narcissism and Self-Centered Behavior

Self-confidence is important for us and our partner. Sometimes, an inflated ego can look like confidence, when in reality, it's a form of narcissism. When someone is a narcissist, they tend to put themselves and their interests above everyone else, including the closest people to them. They may be superficial, self-centered and only truly care about how things impact them, with no regard how other people feel. They may say or do hurtful things, without any pause for reflection and without guilt. Any signs of these characteristics are a good enough reason to leave the relationship.

No Communication

Toxic people may be fun at the beginning of the relationship, though once they become attached to you, they may stop communicating effectively. In fact, they may not be good at communicating at all, only looking to get what they can out of a relationship without having to make any commitment or maintaining a healthy level of connection. When our partner gives us the silent treatment, it is a form of emotional abuse, and it can be very isolating. It's also passive- aggressive, where the impact of being ignored and treated as though we are not important is aggressive, though it is done in a passive nature. Any avoidance of communicating is a bad sign.

Avoidance of responsibility

Partnerships and friendships are built on mutual respect, trust and looking out for one another. When people shirk responsibilities in a relationship, they might not feel that they have to explain themselves if they say or do something hurtful or feel that they bear no responsibility towards mistreating you if they become abusive. In partnerships where both people live together, avoidance of responsibility may include not paying some of the bills or picking up after themselves, leaving their partner to do all or most of the work. It's not an equal relationship and should be avoided at all costs.

Lack of Self-control

If your partner or friend spends too much money all the time, without any regard for their expenses, or financial responsibility, this is a bad sign. They may also lack control in other areas, such as chasing after someone else for intimacy when they are already in a relationship, using alcohol and/or drugs often and with no regard for how using effects them or other people in their life.

A Lack of Respect

In general, many of the traits already covered (above) highlight a lack of respect towards you and your relationship. Even if you manage to convince yourself that other things about the person can be overlooked this is one item that shouldn't be ignored. If a person doesn't respect you, then it is not a healthy relationship and never will be. Signs of disrespect include ignoring you, making insults, using your good nature and generosity in their favor without returning any favors.

There are many other signs for toxic people, which can

include constant drama associated with having them in your life, making you feel worthless, while feeling entitled and better than everyone else. Sometimes, there are people in our life that fit some or all of these criteria, and it's not always possible to avoid them. They may be a relative, co-worker or a boss. In this case, there are ways to address them and make sure we minimize their effect on us.

Handling Toxic People and Setting Boundaries

Setting boundaries is the most important thing to remember when dealing with toxic and narcissistic people. They will often try to pass those boundaries, though setting and reinforcing them is the best way to deal with toxic people and their problems. We may encounter toxic people in more than one part of our life, such as a family member, an employer or supervisor or neighbor. In all these relationships or connections, we may try to avoid them as much as possible, which is generally the best plan. It's not always possible, and for this reason, there are methods and tools we can use to set boundaries and keep them strong when dealing with difficult people.

Setting Boundaries at Work

Establishing a boundary is, in effect, a way to "draw a line" that acts as a limit, and anything beyond that point is unacceptable. Simply stating that "I have to draw the line at this" or "This is far as I can go, the rest is up to you or_____" This is a polite, but firm and professional way to let someone know they can count on you to get the job done, but only within your abilities and scope of work.

Once they push beyond this boundary or line, it's hard to push them back over the line and re-establish that limit. Setting up the initial boundaries, before anyone has a chance to push or "test" you, are the best way for success on the job and setting the expectations for others right away:

Identify your limits. At what point will you become uncomfortable or uneasy? For some people, physical boundaries are very important. Some people may welcome a handshake, a pat on the back, or even a hug, where others do not feel comfortable with any physical contact at all. When we approach other people in these situations and wish to avoid contact, we can be fun or playful by saying something like "I'm not a hugger or handshake person, but let's fist-bump or high-five".

Taking it in stride and being upfront right away, will make people realize it's not on them, but rather your own personal preference. Other limits we may identify include social interaction; some people are eager to start friendships at work, whereas others may want to keep an arms' length distance, treating co-workers as such and nothing more. For others, attending an occasional party or going out for drinks is acceptable, provided we don't get too personal, as this would be crossing the line. Maintaining work relationships is a delicate balance; we want to foster meaningful acquaintances and good relationships with co-workers and colleagues while keeping it professional

Take note on your feelings and reactions. Also, observe how other people behave and act around us. We may notice that some people are good at establishing their own boundaries and respecting ours, even if they are not aware of our limits, but simply show respect and restraint. We can do the same when communicating with other people and watch for cues from them of what is acceptable or not. This is where body language and

non-verbal cues can play a significant role in giving us hints about whether a person wants to engage further in a conversation or not. We can use the same cues or simply state our feelings when we come across an uncomfortable situation: "I'm not comfortable discussing this topic," or "I'd rather stick to (work project or task) instead, is that ok? Talking about this makes me nervous."

_Get familiar with your environment. Understanding the needs of others and the nature of the work culture and people can make setting up boundaries easier. In some work environments, the culture is highly restrictive with specific behavior, dress code and other limits that may seem undesirable for people looking for a more casual atmosphere. For some people, establishing "no physical contact" rules or requiring specific attire or uniforms can make the boundaries easy, as some are already in place. This may not stop some people from trying to cross the line, and this is where becoming familiar with not only company policy, but the types of people working there, can be a good way to know when your limits can be challenged. In other work environments, the atmosphere is relaxed, and people generally get personal or familiar quickly. While this may be a more desirable place to work, without too much restriction and more flexibility, establishing boundaries can be a challenge, as some people easily "blur" the lines between their personal and professional lives. When we draw the line with work colleagues and business contacts, it's straight-forward because the nature of our connection with them is a professional, formal one. Even if we meet them for coffee or enjoy an occasional meal together, the established parameters of how we behave and communicate with them are well established and respected.

Setting Boundaries with Family and Friends

Personal relationships are more difficult when it comes to setting boundaries, as they involve certain people that we are already close to by family or friendship. When we are close to someone, even a spouse or partner, we know more about them (and they about us) then a co-worker or colleague would. For this reason, there may be no boundaries set up at all. This can give some people, specifically toxic or abusive people, an advantage when there are no limits established. We often don't even consider setting a boundary, unless something drastic happens, like an abuse of power or a major conflict that causes grief. Everyone experiences familial conflicts and difficulty in friendships, which puts us in a position to re-evaluate the relationship and determine how genuine it is. Setting the boundaries should be done sooner than later, to establish the "house rules" that you expect, including respect and dignity, which you agree to show in return:

Be clear on how you set your boundaries. Communicate with family and friends by stating it clearly. If you experience a serious argument, after which no one speaks to each other, and later want to reconcile, setting new limits is a powerful way to protect yourself and well-being from further conflict, and will make it clear that certain behaviors are not to be tolerated. For example, you might state the following:

"I want to reconcile, but there is only so much I will tolerate. Please understand and respect my limits."

"I forgive you and want things to improve between us. There are some things that I have to explain first...."

Speak up when someone crosses the line immediately.

Do not let it slide, even if it seems more convenient to do so. In some cases, we may be in a public event or among other family and friends, where confronting someone on their behavior can be frowned upon. In this scenario, it is a personal decision, though the sooner the offending person is confronted about their behavior, the better. Approaching them individually after the event, if you are comfortable in doing so, may be a good way to call them on their actions and explain that they are not tolerated. For some reason, a person may use the public or presence among family to get away with an acceptable action, knowing very well that other people will not feel comfortable confronting them. In this scenario, you have a choice: leave the area and get some fresh air, removing yourself from a toxic situation. The other option: confront the person in a polite, but direct manner, so that they know and understand that you are not afraid to stand up to them and will call them on their actions. This can go in your favor or cause further division within a group. Be prepared that the outcome may not be well received, but it will make your boundaries absolute. It takes courage to stand up for our self, especially when social situations are challenging to begin with. We may even tremble when we speak but doing so is sometimes the only way to establish a limit and enforce the expectation of respect.

When all else fails, avoid toxic family. It's not going to be easy avoiding them, especially if they live close to us, but the alternative is often tolerating abusive traits and behavior that are not acceptable. For this reason, make a point to keep the contact minimal at family gatherings, such as weddings and birthday parties, while maintaining the distance. Avoidance is the last and final step in eradicating the negative impact of toxic people in our lives. We may need to explain to other people in our family and/or social circle that ceasing contact with a specific person is needed for our mental and emotional well-being. Some people may support and understand the decision, while others may not. The most important outcome is that you fair better as a result of ridding your life of toxic people as much as possible.

Making Changes to How we Interact with People and Avoiding Conflict

Some people enjoy conflict. They like to pick a fight, even when there is nothing to argue about or debate. This can be a challenging personality to deal with, especially when experiencing social anxiety in regular situations is challenging for some people. People who like to fight are looking for drama and often possess the traits of a bully with an abusive nature. Sometimes the types of people who like conflict prefer to debate or discuss a topic and may not realize how to approach the situation without antagonizing others. In this way, we can possibly use their interests to advantage, by addressing their need for conflict head-on:

"Are you looking for a fight? Every time we talk, you want to argue. Is there something on your mind that you want to share? I'm ready to listen."

This method of responding may quickly diffuse the other person's tension, when they realize that you are not fighting against them, but rather, on their side and willing to listen. Some people look for a fight when other aspects of their life feel unfulfilling or dull. As confident as they may appear, people who start conflict are looking to fill a gap by ignited others to fight them. It's unhealthy, and it can be destructive, though once they become aware, they are presented with a choice:

a)   They can continue to egg other people on, starting a "fight", without regard for what anyone else says or does.

b)   They may back down, once they know that they will be heard and taken seriously. This may be the one thing they lack most in life: being listened to and understood. While we may not always understand a person's reasons for acting a certain way, they can be easier to communicate with once they feel that we care enough to listen.

When we are faced with a situation involving conflict, we may want to hide our true feelings, to become avoidant. It may be easier to avoid some people altogether. In situations where there is abusive behavior, which can escalate an become dangerous, avoidance is the best option. In other situations, conflict is an obstacle that we can help someone else overcome when we are ready.

For some people thriving on conflict, they may be oblivious to how their actions impact others and instead focus on the energy that comes from the fight. It may help to bring your feelings and thoughts to their attention so that they are aware of the impact their conflict makes:

Explain that when they raise their voice or otherwise bring up a delicate or difficult topic, it makes you feel nervous and unhappy. If they care about how you feel, they will evaluate their actions.

Ask why they want to fight. What is eating them? They may not even be aware that you notice this about them, and they may be unaware that their behavior stems from something else.

Do they want to debate a topic respectfully and civilly? This may be the ultimate opportunity for them, but they have no idea how to start a debate. Some people see debates as a fight of sorts, though debating a topic should be more civil, giving equal consideration to all sides of the argument.

CHAPTER 7

BUILD A STABLE GROUP

OF FRIENDS

Enjoying Solitude for Self-Reflection

As we learn to overcome shyness and social anxiety, we may look for new ways to become engaged with other people and communicate more. It's also healthy and important to realize the benefits of solitude and "alone time". Meaningful conversations, bonding with people and networking is very important, though we don't often take enough time for ourselves to recharge and rejuvenate. Solitude and self-care are valuable for keeping our mind and emotional health in check. It's a way to get in touch with our innermost thoughts and feelings, without the distractions of everyday life. When we release from everything and everyone, even if just for a couple of hours each week, we will experience a sense of renewal and improved self-esteem.

Solitude is a good way to get to know the closest person to us, our selves. Giving our mind and body space to reflect and grow is an important way to achieve a lot of positive action and improvements within, including:

Learning to appreciate our own company. Some people are afraid to be alone, and crave the comfort of others, though the result can be too much dependence. Giving yourself that little bit of space every now and again is a way to release from the daily grind and pressures that we feel in our life.

Try a new hobby or activity that you can do on your own. This can be something active, such as cycling or skating, or an art project. This will give you a chance to "escape" from a busy life while giving yourself a chance to learn something new and fulfill a sense of accomplishment.

Self Esteem & Self Help

Practicing meditation and self-reflection at least once daily for ten or fifteen minutes is a good way to feel grounded and refocused.

Taking a yoga class and learning mediation are valuable ways of exercising and relaxing our mind and body together.

Making time for our self is not as easy as we think when we consider all of the things that can interrupt us at any time. Taking a five-minute break at work could be quickly interrupted, or an afternoon nap at home may end when there are kids and/or family constantly around. Taking a walk alone or finding a space free of distraction is preferred.

144

Meeting People and Finding Healthy Environments for Making New Connections

Making new friends and networking can be a challenge for anyone with social anxiety. When we consider how other people see us, we may think excessively about the negative, and not realize that other people may find us interesting once we get to know them. There are other people with similar interest and common goals, we just have to meet them. With more people meeting online, in social groups and forums where they are essentially "grouped" together by their views, interests, favorite films, celebrities, and other topics, it's not only easier to meet people in general, but with specific common traits. Some people prefer to meet others in person, whether they know them from online first, or meet them in a class or volunteer group.

The key is to meet people doing the same things we like and enjoy, to increase the chances they will enjoy our

145

company and want to converse with us. There are some great places for people:

_Local street and art festivals. This can be a great way to find people interested in the arts and related topics. You may be an artist looking for like-minded creative people to network with or start a friendship. This can be a great way to showcase your own talent if you choose to participate in a similar festival :

Social justice and/or rallies for advocacy. This is becoming a popular way to meet people who share the same values and principles we have on certain issues. Not only are we engaging with a cause we feel strongly about, but we are also meeting others who feel strongly enough to do the same.

Meeting people at work. While keeping professionalism on the job is most important, starting a new friendship can be a rewarding experience, especially if you find someone who is taking a similar career path or have a similar interest. This can be a life-long or career-long connection, which can be very rewarding.

Volunteering for an organization that you feel positive or passionate about can be a way to meet other people who share the same drive. There are many non-profit organizations, shelters, and community centers looking for volunteers all year round. If you are looking to increase your confidence, this can also help by giving you a sense of purpose, by contributing to your community.

When meeting new people, always make sure you get acquainted with them in line with the same way in which you meet. For example, if you are passionate about animal rights, and volunteer for an animal shelter, you may meet someone who shares the same compassion for pets. Getting to know them should begin with the commonalities, such as feelings about animal's rights and similar issues, instead of asking personal questions or getting too personal about your own life. This can put some people off, who may not be interested, or wish to take more time to get familiar with you before they reveal more about themselves.

Navigating Social Media, Websites and Forums Where Online Friendships, Communication Begins

The internet is part of our daily lives. We communicate just as much, if not more, with other people by instant messaging, texting, sharing recipes, posting pictures and opinions online. For people who are usually shy or find social situations difficult, meeting other people online can take the pressure off considerably. In a chat room or forum, people don't have to reveal their true identity, which creates anonymity for many people who feel more comfortable expressing their views and ideas. Social media, while more identifiable, allows people to network faster and more effectively for job opportunities, finding events and festivals that they can attend or simply find other people that they share lots in common with. When networking through social media, we may come across people we don't know, who want to "invite" us into their lives. It's always best to check if they are acquainted with other friends and/or family first. Never feel pressured to communicate or connect with someone who makes us feel uncomfortable or unsafe. Taking precautions online should be no different than how we take the same approach in real life, or offline.

Websites and forums are more informational in nature, especially websites, though they almost always have a link to a social media platform or forum, where we can communicate. This is helpful in finding people who share the same interests, as they will join specific groups online for further conversation and discussion. Forums are a great way to join people with a specific topic, question or concept. This can sometimes provoke a lot of different responses. Some people are more "vocal" online than in person, choosing the internet as a safe space or means to communicate ideas and opinions that they may not feel comfortable sharing with family or friends.

Transitioning from Online to Offline: Building a Connection and Networking Outside of the Internet

Meeting someone for the first time can be nerve-wracking for anyone, especially when we are not sure how they will interact with us. If we meet someone online first, we may think we know them well, especially if pictures are exchanged and their conversations and ideas seem consistent, positive and appealing. Meeting someone from the internet should be taken seriously, as with any new person you encounter (online or offline), and taking measures to protect your safety and expectations should be planned in advance:

Meet in a public area, preferably a coffee shop or café where you can easily exit or leave if you feel uncomfortable. If the person you are meeting is agreeable and accepting of this, it's a good sign. You might want to offer several places to meet, giving them a choice, so that it becomes more of a mutual decision. Does he/she/they look the same as their online picture? If not, did they mention that they may appear older and/or different in person due to using older pictures online? If not, take note and proceed with caution. While some people are self-conscious about their appearance, using older, outdated photos that depict them as much younger can be deceptive to others. If someone looks completely different than their pictures online, leave immediately. It's possible that it may not be the same person, or an account was hacked and used to lure you into meeting with them. Some people are set up to be attacked and robbed if they are seen as vulnerable. Make sure the person you meet is the same person online, otherwise, leave at once. Don't leave the public space to go to their place. It's a risky move that could be considered dangerous if you don't know the person. Knowing someone online is not the same as knowing them in person. If they are insistent that you should visit their home, or go with them to a more secluded place, this is a red flag and should be avoided.

_Let someone know where you will be so that they know

when to expect you will arrive home. Plan on contacting them at a certain time, so they know you are safe, and especially once the date is over, so they can rest assured that you are ok. This is very important for your safety, as a backup should the worst-case scenario occur. As rare as this may be, it doesn't hurt to let a close friend or family know, even if they may not agree with our choice of meeting someone from the internet.

Being safe and cautious is most important, and having a good experience is also very important. Most people who meet in person from online have relatively uneventful or mildly pleasant experiences. Sometimes the person we meet online may seem more exciting and adventurous until we find out that they are not as eager to try new things, but only talk about them. Some people are more talk than action, and this will usually show itself in time. Keep in mind that many of the same points apply to meeting someone for a first date, whether they were first encountered online or not.

1.   Don't set high expectations. Some people will try to impress you online and give you their best. While this is commendable, it's not likely that they will live up to these expectations. Just go with the flow and enjoy their company. They may pleasantly surprise you with other attributes that are fun. Overall, don't expect someone to sweep you off your feet and fall in love. Think of the first date as a new start that may or may not progress.

2.   Arrive on time. Make a strong first impression. Being late, unless there is a good reason, is not a good idea. It gives the impression that you don't value the meeting and see it as an afterthought. Some people will chronically date others from online, not taking many of the dates seriously. Do not give the impression that they are wasting their time with you, or it's going to end the date badly. Arriving early, on the other hand, gives you a chance to relax and take an opportunity to reduce your stress level by becoming familiar with a new restaurant or coffee shop before your date arrives.

3.   Don't get too personal. This can be a disaster for anyone, regardless of how sincere you are (or they are). People who talk too much about past relationships or drama are not going to give you a good experience. You may tolerate some brief reference to an ex-girlfriend or ex-husband, but a constant banter about how they "wronged" you and ruined your life is a big red flag. It may seem like they are genuine, but when a person is fixated on their past relationships, it can mean one or more of the following:

a.   They are still in a relationship and looking for a way out. They may dread the thought of being alone or single and look for someone else to replace the current partner or relationship. If you suspect this is the case, avoid them in the future, or leave.

b.   They are abusive. Anyone who talks badly about a person they profess to have loved dearly is not being entirely honest, nor are they being fair to you. If they just met you, talking about their exes or past relationships should be "off the table". They may be playing the victim and looking for sympathy and see you as a way to "dump" their emotional baggage.

c.   They are not a good fit for a relationship. Getting to know someone, especially after you first meet them, should focus on just that, not going backwards into the past. Positive people who want to make a difference in life will focus on the future, not the past. They will learn from their mistakes and move on, not dwell on them.

4.   Take it easy and listen. Get to know the other person's thoughts and interests. This may be easier than you think if you have already shared a lot of information online together. Listening to them can give you an idea of not just what they say but how. Meeting them in person gives you a chance to observe their non- verbal cues and mannerisms, which is unavailable online.

5.	Be yourself. Dress well, but don't overdo it if you normally wouldn't. Show who you are, give a piece of your personality in what you wear. Just be you and don't try to impress. Making yourself appear differently that who you are is a form of deception and should be avoided. Just as some people may deceive by using older photos of themselves, avoid giving someone the impression that you are someone you are not.

For example, if you are normally quiet and lightly conversational, keep it that way. You are communicating and it can work for you. If you suddenly become loud and bold, it will detract from the authentic you and could make your date uncomfortable. If you are considered a bit unconventional in your topics of conversation or fashion, and your date already knows and accepts this, then go with it. Don't be afraid to be who you are. It's who your date should see in the first place.

6.   Be sincere. Don't overreact or pretend to be interested in sports or natural disasters if they bore you. Some people make the assumption that everyone follows certain sports teams, rooting for one team or another, where some people are completely uninterested and even unfamiliar with team sports altogether. Unless your date is already aware of your interests and the items that do not interest you, take a moment to let them know. Keep it light and fun: "I think sports are excellent, but I just don't follow them." Be upfront about your feelings, and let your date know what you are comfortable talking about.

7.   Don't get too personal. Even if you feel very comfortable and enjoy the first date, don't let your guard down. They are still a new person in your life and giving them too much information about your life can either make them uncomfortable or give someone more information about you than they should have. Protect your identity, if you don't use your full name online, and instead, use just your first name.

8.   Set the expectations. Let them know that you have boundaries and limitations on a first date. If you expect more or less, communicate this as well. It doesn't hurt to explain the limits right away, so there are no misunderstandings later. Making your intentions or expectations clear should be done in a relaxed, and friendly manner: "I'm available for the next two hours, but then I have to go, is that ok?" Wait for their response. If they feel that you owe them more time or have more expectations, without communicating these thoughts beforehand, exercise caution. This could mean that they do not have the best intentions. Most people are accepting, and happy for the opportunity to meet. It's also a good idea to remind them that if all goes well, you'd like to see them again.

David Cooper

CHAPTER 8

PSYCHOLOGY AND SELF-IMPROVEMENT

You probably already know that psychological principles are widely applied for self-improvement purposes. If you are like most people, there are definitely several areas in your life that you would like to improve. Maybe you want to be more organized, to give up junk food, to take up an exercise regimen, to improve your performance at work or at school, or to just live a more fulfilled life. The changes that you need to make in your life are going to be difficult and challenging, and you may need to rewire your brain in order to find the willpower or the motivation to take action to make those changes. That is where positive psychology comes in. Psychologists these days do not just focus on issues that are clinically significant—

these days, psychological principles can be applied anywhere and to anyone in order to realize specific self-improvement goals.

The first step towards self-improvement is self-awareness. We discussed self-awareness earlier in this book when we talked about developing emotional intelligence. If you want to be more self-aware, you have to take stock of your sensations, your thoughts, your emotions, and your behavioral patterns. The reason we find it hard to start new positive habits is that we have certain emotions, thoughts, and behaviors that we have become accustomed to, so our brains will tend to resort to those old habits and resist attempts to develop new ones. When we take stock of our current psychological state, we will be in a better position to figure out what areas need change, and why we are reluctant to embrace new habits. You can take stock of your psychological state by keeping a journal for at least a couple of weeks, and then consciously reviewing all your tendencies and convictions to see which ones are inhibiting your ability to make progress in your life. Your goal, in this case, is to understand the things that limit you, and to identify the psychological chains that bind you, and stop you from achieving your self-improvement goals.

Ways to Improve Your Mindset

To achieve self-improvement, you first need to improve your mindset. Psychologists define the term mindset as a belief or a system of beliefs that orient the way a person approaches certain situations. Your mindset determines the way you perceive certain events and the way you select and execute a certain course of action in order to achieve a very specific goal. A positive mindset can help you see opportunities that are hidden, while a negative mindset can trap you in a cycle of self-defeating thoughts and behaviors and stop you from making any real progress. As much as possible, you should avoid having a fixed mindset. The reason we have gone into so much detail in this book to explain the principles of psychology and the working mechanisms of the brain, is to make it possible for you to understand that the human mind isn't a fixed thing and that it can be trained to think in certain ways, resulting in certain behavioral modifications. People who do not understand the basics of psychology tend to assume that their abilities are innate and therefore their failure in certain areas of life cannot be prevented or reversed.

A lot of people think that they are just "not good at math" or that they just "can't do public speaking." You have seen in this book how the brain learns, and how it processes thoughts, memories, and emotions, so you understand that you are fully capable of changing your brain has thought patterns by using repetition and reinforcement as a learning technique. You know that the brain is not a rigid thing, so you understand that you are fully capable of changing your mindset if you work hard on it.

Do not be preoccupied with perfection. To have a positive mindset, you have to be less concerned with doing things perfectly and more concerned with making progress and making gradual improvements. If you are preoccupied with doing something perfectly and eliminating all errors, you are more likely to be stuck where you are, and to be afraid of taking steps to change your situation out of the fear of committing errors.

Supposing you want to start exercising in order to improve your health and fitness. Your priority should be to get started as soon as possible and to make improvements as you go. You should not wait for the perfect conditions to get started. If you wait to find the perfect gym, the perfect outfit, the perfect instructor, or the perfect time, you may never get around to doing any exercise. The point is that perfection is an illusion, and looking for perfect conditions is just another way to procrastinate.

To improve your mindset, you need to learn patience. In most things that we undertake, it may take some time before we begin to see real results. If you have a well thought out plan and you have put it into action a few times, but you have not yet seen the results you have been hoping for, it does not mean you should give up immediately. Many people who go on self-improvement journeys expect to see instant result. If you are trying to pick up a positive habit, say for example you are trying to have a healthier morning routine, you have to understand that you are essentially overwriting years or even decades of old habits in your brain, so it may take some time before the new habit feels more natural to you.

How to Be More Optimistic in Your Outlook

To learn optimism, you have to acknowledge your pessimism. You have to consciously go through your pessimistic ideas and analyze them, then challenge all the negative assumption that you are making. When you identify your negative assumption, you may be able to see the error in the pessimistic conclusions that you are drawing. Even when we are pessimistic, we do not want to be called pessimists, but for this to work, assume that every negative thought you that have comes from a place of pessimism and not from an objective assessment of the situation.

In conflict resolutions, the two parties are often told to start by saying something positive about each other. You can apply the same trick to become more optimistic. For every situation that you find yourself in, try to have one positive thought about that situation no matter how negative it may be. Even if the positive thought does not ring true at the time, try to have it anyway. Let us say you get out of the house in the morning, and you realize someone stole your car. There may be no apparent upside to that situation, but you should try to dig deep and find one, even if it is a weak one. For instance, you can decide to think of it as an opportunity to get a new car (even if it is going to cost you). The point of this kind of exercise is not to turn you into a "blind optimist." It is to stop you from being habitually negative.

You can form the habit of searching for positive aspects in all kinds of negative situations, and you can even turn it into a little game that you play in your mind. Did your date go horribly wrong? Well, at least you had the chance to dine in a fancy restaurant. Were you fired from your job? Well, it is a chance to search for a new and perhaps even better job that fulfills you. Were you dumbed? Well, it's a chance to find someone whom you are more compatible with.

You can also think of someone you may know who always has a positive outlook, and try to imagine what they would have thought if they were in your situation. It can be anyone real (e.g., a friend or relative you admire, a historical figure, a famous person, a religious or spiritual figure, etc.) or even fictional (e.g., a character in your favorite movie, television series, book, comic book, etc.). For example, if you have to give a presentation to a group of people and your fear of public speaking creeps up, you can ask yourself "What would Abraham Lincoln thing or do in this case?" Honest Abe was pathologically shy, but he overcame his fear to deliver one of the greatest and most consequential speeches in history. If he could do that, then you could get yourself to keep it together for the duration of a PowerPoint presentation.

Finally, to become more optimistic, you must learn to practice optimism as often as you can. You have to overhaul your entire outlook in life, and you will not be able to accomplish that if you are ineffective in your approach. You must take every chance that you can to practice optimism and to sharpen your positive mindset. Your brain may be an "old dog," but from what you have learned in this book, it is fully capable of learning new tricks, as long as you keep reinforcing those lessons.

CONCLUSION

Activities and Hobbies to Improve Communication

When we become more confident in our abilities and level of communication, it's advantageous to find ways to continually improve and maintain a healthy level of focus. Strategy, dialogue, and self-improvement are all life-long pursuits that keep us mentally and emotionally strong and healthy. Try some of the following games, hobbies and activities to keep your mind, confidence and communication skills sharp:

Chess, checkers and similar strategy games

Playing chess is an excellent way to develop strategy and planning skills. Chess easy to assemble, and while learning to play can take some time, it's a worthwhile skill that greatly benefits your ability to see a situation from a "big picture" view, while observing the details, looking ahead several moves before making a move. Chess is a great mental workout for all ages, and there are often chess clubs and tournaments that provide an option for people to learn to play or develop their skills for various levels in competition. Checkers, puzzles and word game are excellent for developing creativity and critical thinking skills, similar to chess, only with different criteria

.

Knitting, Needlepoint, and Crafts

Taking up a new hobby can be a great way to relieve stress and find a new way to be creative. Some studies indicate that knitting, crochet and similar forms of needlework can reduce anxiety and stress, and even improve mood and symptoms of people who suffer from depression. Making a new project can also give us a sense of satisfaction and a renewed sense of worth. It's another way to discover a hidden talent that we didn't realize we possessed until we put it to use.

Martial arts and Yoga

Balancing your mind and body, while keeping in good physical shape goes a long way to maintaining good levels of confidence and even increasing our positive outlook on our self and others. Martial arts are very goal-oriented and can help improve our self-discipline, leading to better time management and an overall sense of self-worth.

Reading a book (fiction or non-fiction)

Take time to read one or two books a month, at the very least, and add to your mental "library". Learning about an author and becoming familiar with his or her work can be an excellent conversation piece at a social event.

Some people may share their own reviews or critiques of the same books you enjoy and may also offer recommendations of their own. For example, if you enjoy dystopian fiction, but only know one or two authors, you may find that a discussion about the topic will bring up many more references and books that imagined. Reading non-fiction is another way to learn more about the world we live in. Even when we are in social circles that don't enjoy discussion of books, reading, in general, is good for our vocabulary and diction. We can expand not only the words we use, though using them to better express our thoughts and ideas when we are in a conversation.

Public Speaking and the Advantages of Learning to Speak in Front of a Crowd

People are always conquering fears and phobias, including social anxiety and the fear of communication with others. Even in the most successful situations, including people without any fear of socializing at all, public speaking can be a source of anguish and dread. The very idea of standing in front of a large group of people to address them stops a lot of people from entering certain types of work where public speaking is part of the job.

There are advantages to learning how to speak in front of a group, even if it makes you nervous:

It gives you a new experience. Not everyone can or is willing to speak in front of a crowd (they won't even try). Adding a skill such as public speaking to your basket of skills is valuable, even if you don't plan on using it.

It's a good way to see how people respond to you. Write everything down, and don't expect to commit everything to memory, especially if what you have to say is involving. Focus on your posture, take a deep breath and do your best.

Being nervous in front of a crowd is completely normal and most people have experienced it with public speaking. It's a new skill you can develop if you decide that it's not as bad or negative as you imagined. Public speaking can be a way to face your social anxiety head-on. Sometimes doing the very things that scare us or make us afraid can give us the boost we need to conquer the fear and work more on self-improvement.

It can make talking to smaller groups of people easier. Once you've stood up in front of a large crowd or group of people, speaking up in a smaller group will seem less intimidating. You may notice a better comfort level in a smaller group as well, and speaking, expressing yourself will be less awkward and flow more smoothly.

You will make new friends and acquaintances. Not everyone enjoys public speaking, and when they see you giving it a try, they may develop a lot more respect for you and our efforts. You may encounter people approaching you after, giving you their approval and thoughts on how you did. Some people may offer constructive criticism, which is also beneficial, and usually done with good intentions. From this experience, you may discover new people to connect with, even a hidden talent, which would be very beneficial for improving your social skills!

Avoiding Negativity and Proactively Promoting a Positive Outlook

As long as we see only the negative side of life, it can be difficult to appreciate and focus on positivity. When we read the news or hear other people's gossip or criticisms, it's so easy to fall into a negative zone where all we think of is the worst of humanity. We often forget that most news items have a negative spin, or are about celebrities, sports, and public figures, and not about us in our everyday life. We can make our own positivity by the way we act.

Being proactive, learning to adapt to different situations (and people), and looking for solutions instead of dwelling on problems are all ways in which we can promote a more positive outlook in life for ourselves and others. One such example is a lady (Alice) who was not happy with her physical appearance and wanted to quit smoking. She worked in a warehouse, where many people often gave her judgmental glances, occasionally telling her she needs to eat less and go to the gym. As hurtful as it was, she ignored them mostly, until she worked up the courage to state "have a good day too" or "would you like to become my personal trainer, then?" Eventually, the rude comments died down, and Alice continued with her job. She tried quitting smoking, which took some time, but she did it. After six months, her breathing improved greatly and she decided to take the stairs at work, instead of an elevator. With renewed confidence in feeling better internally, Alice decided to walk the entire building, every shift break, instead of the usual smoke break. This caused a lot of people to take notice, even the same individuals who made nasty comments and judgmental glances. In addition to walking, Alice begins cycling to work and trying other forms of fitness.

Some forms for exercise were not a good fit, but she made an effort and eventually stuck with cycling and walking.

One day a co-worker took notice of Alice walking around the building and approached her to express how much she respected her progress. Alice jokingly mentioned that at least no one insults her anymore, so that's worth the effort in itself. The co-worker responded with the following statement:

"People change how they perceive you when you strive to make improvements in yourself"

It wasn't Alice's weight loss and improved appearance that stopped the negativity, nor was it because she exercised more. She had nothing to prove to anyone else and made the improvements for her own benefit. When people make an effort to better themselves and strive forward, other people, whether they say anything or not, take notice. Any misperceptions made before have since changed. How many people are judged by their appearance or status in life?

Keeping it Positive and Knowing Your Value in all forms of Social Interactions

Improving social skills will always be linked to how we view our selves and maintaining a positive outlook and working on our self-confidence are key factors in helping us approach social engagements and handling difficult situations. The more we know about why we feel inadequate sometimes, or why we fear talking to other people, the more effectively we can target certain points for progress. These quick tips and points of encouragement are good to keep on hand for all types of social situations, and when struggling with self-esteem:

_You have something to offer. It may not seem like we have much to say in some social situations, where others may appear to know more about certain topics. Even if this is the case, there will be at

least one item that we know more about than someone else, or enough to offer some advice or interesting facts.

Never underestimate what you already know, and always look to learn something new if you want to improve on your knowledge.

–

Your presence is valued. You may feel ignored sometimes, or it feels this way, within a group of people. This doesn't mean that they are purposely avoiding you, but rather, heavily involved in a discussion without paying any attention beyond their circle. Don't be afraid to approach a group, especially if the conversational tone if fun and light-hearted. Certain people may not engage right away for the same reasons we hesitate, though they may be happy once you introduce yourself and become part of the conversation. You have a good sense of humor. This may not be apparent until you find yourself in a conversation about a funny topic, and it ignites something inside of you that you never thought you had – a sense of humor and an ability to make people laugh. A lot of famous comedians began as shy, awkward people until they realized their potential. Sometimes we second guess what we want to say, and instead of taking a risk, we bury it inside.

Humour is a great way to bridge the gap between many different types of people, including people who would normally fight or disagree with each other. A good sense of humor has a way of uniting people, in a way and releasing stress at the same time. A strong, hearty laugh will not only liven up a party or conversation, but it's also good for your confidence and health as well.

You deserve to have a good time. When we avoid social interaction because we fear how others perceive us, not only are we usually wrong about others, we miss out on having a good time and meeting new people. Never deprive yourself of an opportunity to grow and feel good about yourself. Sometimes the quiet person in the room can light up everyone's face when he or she speaks. This can have an amazing effect on how other people view them, and they may see this as an opportunity to get to know you better.

Don't underestimate yourself. People want to hear from you and what you have to say. Never assume that you are unimportant, even if you feel this way. At the very least, challenge your thoughts and put yourself "out there" to discover new places, people and things. Life is about discovery and learning. The more we realize how much there is to learn and overcome, the better we become at it. Finally, have fun! Socializing at work, school, with family or at any event should be fun, not a something to avoid or fear. When we experience conflict, we can use tools and techniques to overcome difficult situations and prevail through them. On average, most conflicts are brief in nature, only lasting second or minutes, and yet some can leave an impression. On the other hand, positive, funny and poignant conversations can go on for hours! Getting through conflict will pave the way towards more meaningful, thoughtful and enjoyable conversation and social interaction that everyone can enjoy.

CPSIA information can be obtained
at www.ICGtesting.com
Printed in the USA
LVHW020054040121
675552LV00009B/311